GARAGE TO THE GLOBE

WITH 51 SIMPLE SUCCESS MANTRAS

By

Ravinder Nath Khanna

Founder & Chairman C&S Electric Ltd

Content Enhanced by Ms Maneesha Agrawal (MVG)

Published by Invincible Publishers

First Printing: 2019

The events are portrayed to the best of the author's recall and understanding. The conversations are not written verbatim. The views and opinions expressed in this book are the author's own and the facts are as reported by him which have been verified to the extent possible, and the publishers are not in any way liable for the same.

ISBN: 978-81-943134-3-4

Invincible Publishers

Registered Address: 201A, SAS Tower, Sector 38,
Gurgaon-122003

Printed at Excel Printers Pvt. Ltd.

I Have A Dream

Dedicated To My Loving Family
Including The Entire C&S Electric Ltd Family.

Dedicated To All Those Starry Eyed Dreamers, Aspirers
Who Want A Quantum Jump In Happiness & Contentment
In Their Lives Ahead.

Dedicated To All Start-Ups And Would Be Start-Ups
Who Attempt Dreaming Big And Succeed.

TABLE OF CONTENT

My Tool Kit of 51 Simple Success Mantras
Your Master Key and Simple Ready Reckoner for
Creating Happier and More Successful Lives Ahead

My Tool Kit of 51 Simple Success Mantras
Your Master Key and Simple Ready Reckoner for
Creating Happier and More Successful Lives Ahead

My Tool Kit of 51 Simple Success Mantras
Your Master Key and Simple Ready Reckoner for
Creating Happier and More Successful Lives Ahead

My Tool Kit of 51 Simple Success Mantras
Your Master Key and Simple Ready Reckoner for
Creating Happier and More Successful Lives Ahead

Chapter 1

Foreword

By

COMMANDER V.K. JAITLY (RETD)

EX PRESIDENT OF THE ALUMNI FOUNDATION, IIT KHARAGPUR
VETERAN AUTHOR COACH AND MANAGEMENT CONSULTANT

Foreword

We are into the seventh decade of our Independence. As a Nation we have come a long way – our premier Institutes the renowned IITs, our business schools and even the most prestigious Universities in India have produced outstanding scholars, Professionals, Engineers, Doctors, Professors, Scientists, Research Scholars and outstanding Managers in each and every faculty and walk of life.

Relatively however very few First Generation Entrepreneurs have so far been produced, who have successfully founded and raised their sizeable own Industries and Enterprises from the very scratch.

Fewer still are those who have brought up their Start-ups to International levels of excellence, recognition and repute in specialized and sophisticated fields. Such as in Power Generation Protection & Control the majority of space is occupied worldwide even today by hardly ten Multinationals only.

Among giants in this field like Siemens of Germany, ABB Switzerland, Schneider France, GE and Eaton of USA, Mitsubishi & Toshiba Japan, LG Korea & Chint of China is also the **C&S Electric** of India founded, raised and promoted by our own IITan of the 1962 batch of Electrical Engineering, Ravi - Ravinder Nath Khanna.

RAVI is a daring entrepreneur and a dreamer, who dreamt of a tomorrow which was totally different from his family's more than a 100 year old legacy and tradition in the profession of law & judiciary until then, being the son of Late Mr. Justice P. N. Khanna.

Back in 1962, Ravi was campus picked from IIT Kharagpur by Metzeneaur & Jung, Gmbh – a leading German Company in Power Products for technical training. Followed, if successful, with a job of a Design Engineer in their company in Germany.

Such was Ravi's vision, determination and confidence he had

gained that after hardly three years of working and gaining on the job experience in Designing, Manufacturing and Commissioning Sophisticated LV & MV Switchgear Equipment and Systems, he boldly chose to resign from his lucrative job in Germany to return back to his roots in India by the end of 1965 to replicate what he had learned overseas.

This was totally unlike most other of his batch mates and most other Indian Engineers those days who preferred to settle overseas.

Here is a unique story of an IITian, who firmly believed even in the early 1960's what an average Indian with very little means could also accomplish and achieve if he was dedicated and determined.

His tiny garage start-up of 1966 with an initial investment of INR 10,000/- only out of his earnings is the prestigious **C&S Electric Limited** of India today–employing a team of almost 5,000 dedicated technocrats, engineers, professionals and highly skilled in-house trained workmen.

Ravi's **C&S Electric** today is spread over 17 of their manufacturing plants in India and overseas, occupying a well-earned position among the world leaders in Electrical Industry, making the IIT Kharagpur and India proud.

This is a story of passion and pursuit of excellence in entrepreneurship. Such a success story should increasingly be seen read and emulated by most young and even not so young aspirants of all ages today in their own occupations & professions.

You will thoroughly enjoy and immensely benefit reading this rare and highly motivating book, using the unique visualization and the simple success Mantras Tool-Kit technique adopted by Ravi.

Commander V.K. Jaitly (Retd)
Ex President of the Alumni Foundation, IIT Kharagpur
Veteran Author Coach and Management Consultant

At IIT Kharagpur 1961

Ravi - RNK sitting fourth from left as the Secretary General of Electrical Engineering Association at IIT-Kharagpur, 1961 with Prof. Menon, Head of the Department & Prof. Roy Chowdhury & other Office Bearers and students of Electrical Engg.

Since time immemorial, the Lion has been an emblem of India. It Stands for strength courage tenacity and wisdom values that are every bit as Indian Today as they have eve been for 10000 years of Indian civilization.

The wheels denotes peaceful progress and dynamism - a sign from an enlightened pas Pointing the way to a vibrant future.

Spread over 15 Acres, one of our World Class Manufacturing Plants at SIDCUL Haridwar, adjoining BHEL Haridwar

Being one of the largest manufacturers of Electrical Equipment for Power Generation, Transmission, Distribution & Control, not only for the large market in India but also: Being the largest exporters from India, of our world-class products to 85 countries around the globe, Regularly Branding and supplying several of our well known Products for other World Leaders.

Across the Value Chain of
LV Switchgear and Protection
Power Control Components
Contactors, Thermal & Electronic Overload Relays, Pneumatic & Electronic Timers, MPCBs, Motor Starters, Control & Signaling Devices
Power Distribution Components
Switch Disconnectors, Switch Disconnector Fuses, Change Over Switches, HRC Fuses, MCCBs & Air Circuit Breakers
Final Power Distribution Components
MCBs, RCCBs, DBs, Industrial Plugs and Sockets
Protection & Measurement Devices
Multi Functional Relays, Control and Relay Panels
Low Voltage Switchboards
Modular Motor & Power Control Centers, Intelligent PCCs and MCCs
MV Switchgear
Package Substations, Ring Main Units
MV Vacuum Circuit, Breakers & Switchgears
Lighting & Wiring Accessories
LED Indoor Lighting
LED Outdoor Lightir
Modular Switches & Accessories
C&S electric
CELEBRATING 50 YEARS
C&S Electric Ltd

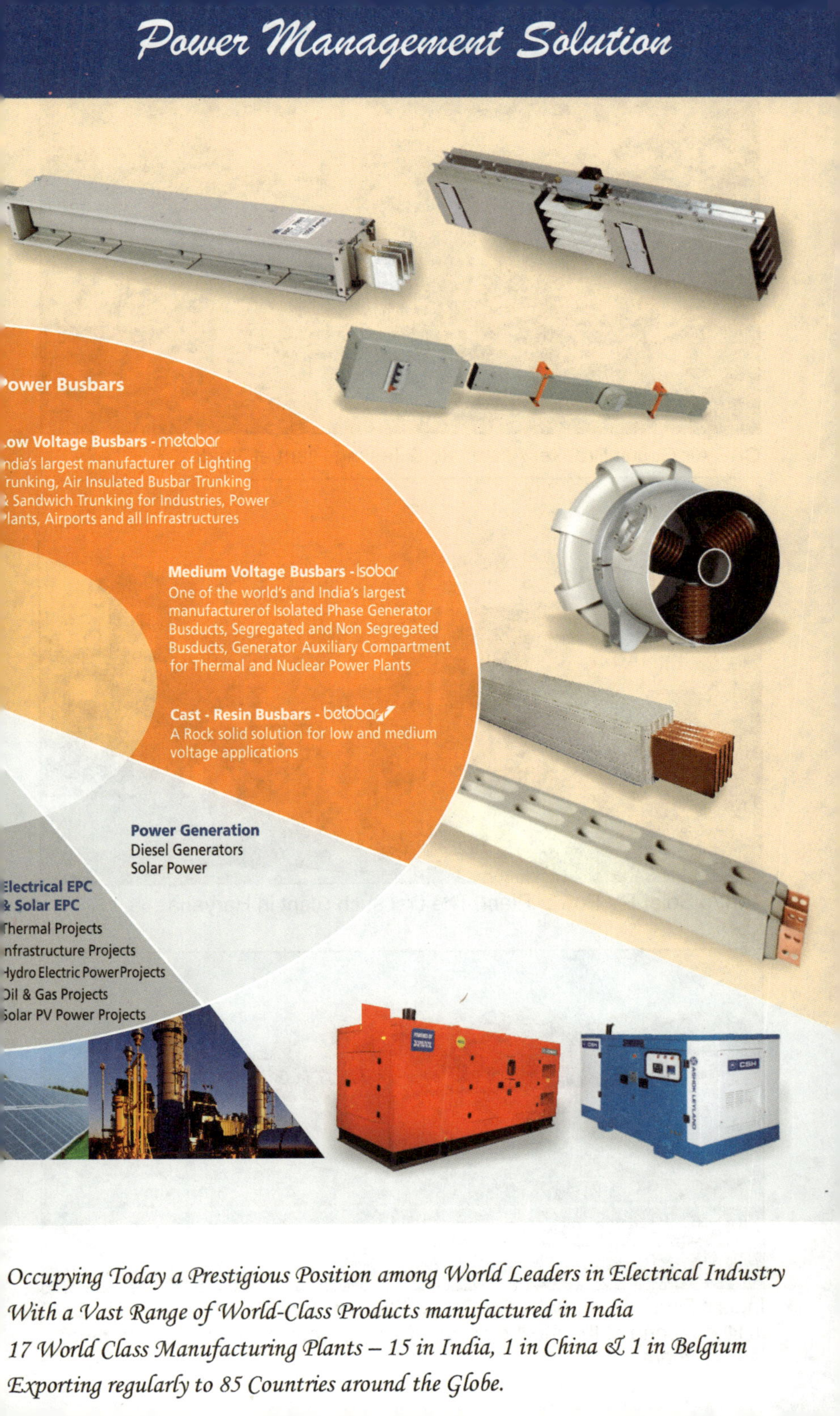
Power Management Solution
ower Busbars
ow Voltage Busbars - metabar
ndia's largest manufacturer of Lighting
runking, Air Insulated Busbar Trunking
Sandwich Trunking for Industries, Power
lants, Airports and all Infrastructures
Medium Voltage Busbars - isobar
One of the world's and India's largest manufacturer of Isolated Phase Generator Busducts, Segregated and Non Segregated Busducts, Generator Auxiliary Compartment for Thermal and Nuclear Power Plants
Cast - Resin Busbars - betobar
A Rock solid solution for low and medium voltage applications
Power Generation
Diesel Generators
Solar Power
lectrical EPC
Solar EPC
hermal Projects
nfrastructure Projects
ydro Electric Power Projects
il & Gas Projects
olar PV Power Projects
Occupying Today a Prestigious Position among World Leaders in Electrical Industry
With a Vast Range of World-Class Products manufactured in India
17 World Class Manufacturing Plants – 15 in India, 1 in China & 1 in Belgium
Exporting regularly to 85 Countries around the Globe.

C&S Air Circuit Breaker Assembly & Testing Plant at Noida

1MWp Solar PV Power Plant, The first such Plant in Haryana.

India's First 1 MWp Solar PV Power Plant at Haryana set up by us in 2008 is till date one of the most efficient of such plants in the country over the last 11 years.

MAKE IN INDIA

50 years of a Dedicated & Successful Make in India - Skill India Mission

OUR VISION

- To make "MADE IN INDIA' a respected label the World over in our Field of Electricals upto 33kV
- To skill Indian Engineers & Workers at par with the Best in the World and to serve as a Role Model to other Indian Companies
- To make C&S as the most trusted, respected and preferred brand
- To be closest to our customers
- To manage power in the Biggest of Thermal, Nuclear, Hydroelectric & Solar Power Plants in all Industries, in the Highest Buildings, in most Critical Infrastructures including Railways and in millions of Homes

OUR MISSION

- To create a unique alchemy of outstanding products, operational excellence, path-breaking customer services and compelling marketing
- To create the best place to work where employees are empowered, cared, developed and provided unlimited opportunities
- To continuously innovate, enhance our core technologies and develop new world-class products
- To be India's largest exporter of industrial power distribution and control equipment
- To everyday experience, the sheer joy of delighting our internal and external customers
- To earn healthy return on investment

OUR VALUES

- Stretch for your customer
- Be frank, be honest
- Be obsessed with quality
- Work hard, smart and swift
- Succeed as a team and as an individual
- Discover your strength and those of others

Chapter 2

A Note of Thanks

By

My Worthy Content Enhancer Ms. Maneesha Agrawal (MVG)

A Note of Thanks

Two years back I received an invite to work on a book. It was to compile the journey of an entrepreneur 'who had dared to dream and make it big'. The enterprise which was created was **Control & Switchgear Limited**. I surfed through the internet, glanced at the company profile and got prepared to meet up the Founder Chairman, Sh. R. N. Khanna.

I first met Ravi Sir at his office where he briefed his thoughts on this project which he was preparing to work by then. He wanted his story to be told, with a sole purpose to inspire the future aspirers.

In that first meeting I got the one formidable impression which lasts for life.

Ravi Sir had a vision, and I have followed. Whether I have been able to enhance his vision or not that is for the readers to judge, but I would not forego this opportunity to add a few words I've always wanted to get conveyed.

To Ravi sir, and his readers.

Some people live and some design living. Some are individuals and some are legends. Ravi sir is a legend who took to redesign living.

His thought process is like a power house generating light for many others to follow the route to their individual success.

Whatever he has learned and earned – he has put forth in shape of this book as his repayment to the society. It is his foresight that his story should reach all aspiring entrepreneurs in order to ignite and rekindle their passion to excel, to supersede their own benchmarks.

I've had this amazing chance to work with him. And what to say – it has transformed my own thinking! A perfectionist that he is, he inspires each cell of my cerebral capacity to be at peak.

The book is not just 'another autobiography' it is an exemplary work. It has the most unique 50 Mantra Tool Kit to assist its readers achieve their own dreams and goals. As Mr Khanna himself says, his purpose of writing this book has been to guide young aspirers and empower young minds. The book has the potential to spark up many more future entrepreneurs. Written in his own style, easy to emulate and friendly fashion besides being replete with relatable photographs it is easily one of the best life story that ever came to the readers.

I take it a privilege to specifically mention Ravi Sir's ever graceful humility that has touched me to the core. I doubt if I could meet someone like him before or after! I consider it rather an extraordinary honour that was extended to me when I was called to work with him.

With all my sincere most regards for him I thank him once again for the positivity his book has brought in my life.

Wishing his Readers all the positivity in life,

- MVG (Maneesha Agrawal)
Writer, Content Enhancer

A brief introduction of the story of my life - the foundation of the Control & Switchgear company now called the C&S Electric Ltd.

- By Ravinder Nath Khanna

Chapter 3

A Brief Introduction Of The Story Of My Life - The Foundation Of The Control & Switchgear Company Now Called The C&S Electric Ltd.

My Dear Young – Younger And Older Readers From All Walks Of Life, Students From Primary Schools & Colleges, Students From All Universities & Faculties, Students From All IITs And Business Schools And All Starry-Eyed Seekers, Aspirers, Pursuers Optimists & Karamyogis

You and I, we are all alike. We all wish to create an honest, dignified and a step by step improving comfortable living standard for ourselves and our families. We also wish to contribute to the rapid growth and betterment of our beloved Country and Countrymen in some way or the other.

Living, for each and every aspiring individual can always be a very interesting, creative, fulsome and rewarding experience– no matter where and under what circumstances one is born into or what profession one is currently engaged with today.

By the Universal Law of Nature, life always reserves and showers a chunk of rewards for each and every young or older aspiring individual under its expanse, INCLUDING YOU.

Opportunities my dear aspirants always come knocking at the doors for all human beings. However and always, it is then incumbent upon each and every individual to recognize encash or ignore those opportunities which life offers to each and every one of us, nevertheless.

My own tryst with destiny, through an overnight compelling uprooting from our age old family Haveli and its comforts in Lahore, then India, to a small rented shelter in far away Mussoorie Hills - India in order to save our lives during the partition of India in 1947 did however trigger my own struggle in my life at an early age of 7 years and 7 months already.

My sincere dreams and deep desire to rapidly rebuild our own uprooted family as also our partitioned country had already yielded some results by the time I was 16 years old in 1956. I had found a new direction and a path to boldly change at least for myself our family's 100 year old legacy until then in Law & Judiciary.

In pursuit of this newly acquired objective I worked relentlessly and was fortunate to qualify through the most difficult and highly contested IIT Entrance Examination for joining the one and only IIT Kharagpur, until then in India.

One such day almost 57 long years ago in 1962, I had graduated with a first class Honors Degree in Electrical Engineering from the reputed IIT Kharagpur.

Like all young aspirers, I had also stepped out in this world to pursue my own dreams and desires. I was intending to search my own share of rewards and opportunities ahead.

And look what a reward I got!

I was campus picked up from the IIT Kharagpur for a challenging job of a Design Engineer in Germany by a reputed German Company Metzenauer & Jung Gmbh – FANAL. They were manufacturing a wide range of sophisticated Electrical & Electronic Equipment for Power Generation, Transmission, Distribution, Protection and Automation.

My own initiative and extra efforts put in choosing to learn the difficult German language which was an option (not compulsion) in my final years at the IIT came as a very handy reward and blessing in disguise – later in my selection by the German Company which also changed the course of my whole life ahead.

After joining my first and exciting new job assignment at the Metzenauer & Jung Gmbh, Wuppertal, Germany my on the job training, further perfection and fluency in German language and the practical exposure were extremely beneficial. They were eye opening and very complementary to the excellent theoretical knowledge already gained at the IIT Kharagpur, India.

A lot of barriers and gaps in understanding that were in my mind however between the theoretical knowledge and the practical exposure were cleared through interactions with my readily helpful German colleagues. This became a highly rewarding and enlightening experience. I had by then thoroughly started enjoying my new assignment as a Design Engineer.

My German Boss appreciated my quick learnings. He also observed the advantage I had over my German colleagues once I became more fluent in the German language besides my own command over English already. Resultantly I was promoted every year and travelled extensively alone and with my Boss in Europe & England on Technical Missions and Seminars that we held for large customers making me more and more confident in my profession.

Within hardly three years, I had already gained adequate design and practical working knowledge and confidence in their extensive and intricate product range.

Despite my lucrative and comfortable job in Germany I was also getting absolutely restless about my craving. My future course of action was to fulfill my dream of starting on my own back home in India.

A consciousness impregnated with a great potential was already beginning to emerge. I had felt packed, infused with some kinesis which was keen to radiate - not knowing how and when.

Finally at my young age of 25 years only therefore, I dared and decided to relinquish and resign from my highly interesting, involving and lucrative job in Germany to enable my return back to my roots in India by October 1965.

My decision to return home with utmost urgency and determination was self-ordained to utilize my freshly acquired German technical knowledge to kick start my own industry in India. It was to be in a field where until then mostly big giants and multinationals like Siemens, ABB, Larsen & Toubro, English Electric, GE, Cutler Hammer Eaton, Telemecanique, Schneider, Toshiba, Mitsubishi etc. used to rule the roost.

Driven by this deep desire, passion and fervor in my own fresh young mind and increasingly realizing that if the disciplined

Germans could rebuild their completely war torn country, their destroyed industry, and their shattered economy after The World War II 'Why can we Indians not do the same in India' – what an opportunity I thought!

Having learnt from the Germans that in the startup of any new business a penny saved is a pound made I chose the lowest available minimal travelling expenses and freight cost back home. I travelled by a 14 day long interesting ship-journey on board the French ship Kamboj from Marseille (in French Riviera) to Bombay, India.

This helped me to bring certain testing tools & tackles and a whole lot of drawings & dossiers I had collected during my working experience besides lots of gifts for the family naturally.

My single handed raised STARTUP of 1966 in the Car Garage of my father's residence back then with a meagre Rs 10,000/- still in my pocket out of my earnings in Germany was duly backed with consistent and relentless step by step efforts over the last 53 long years.

Our C&S Electric Ltd of India is today employing together almost 5000 Technocrats, Professionals and highly skilled Workmen. We are occupying a prestigious position among world leaders in the Electrical Industry with a vast range of world class products manufactured in India in our world class manufacturing plants.

Today we have 15 world class manufacturing plants in India, 1 in China and 1 in Belgium. There is also a recent small new startup in Chicago, USA. We are exporting regularly to 85 Countries around the globe.

By the grace of God and blessings of my revered parents, plus my own step by step consistent efforts I can see that I am standing today where I wanted to be – having worked relentlessly throughout my life span. We can all do it likewise in our own professions. **However, it only requires two things – crystal and stone. A vision that is crystal clear, and a will that is stone hard. It is all completely possible, as you will discover yourself clearly through this book.**

My daunting challenges, successes, failures of the last 53 long years I feel call for a mention now. Also for being chronicled today enabling to share my rewarding experiences with all upcoming, young and older aspirers. My worthy readers can now determine for themselves that how worthwhile the journey of my life has been; and whether there is something in it worth learning and emulating under their specific varying conditions, positions and circumstances in which they may be engaged today.

Without using therefore any complex terminology or the usual too serious and mundane sermons and syllabus normally used in such books, I am simply proceeding as an amateur in book writing with the hope that each and every one of you who reads this book using my simple success Mantra Tool-Kit and the visualization communicating technique explained in straight forward easy language in this book should thoroughly enjoy the experience. You should get inspired and should be a net gainer in life one way or the other.

For some time hereafter, let this book become your constant companion for success and a ready reckoner for all the questions that you may have in your mind on entrepreneurship or for uplifting and betterment of your lives ahead. They should all get answered here.

I do hope that this book and it's deliberately chosen relaxed style, small and crisp write ups and comments bring all the universal good fresh and happy everlasting enthusiasm into your lives and those of your loved ones.

My Dear Readers let me now take you on this wonderful and enlightening flight of discovery - the discovery of your own true potential and happiness in a most enjoyable, doable, simple and systematic way.

Stay Blessed - Loved & Protected
Ravinder Nath Khanna, RNK

Related Family And Company Pictures Over A 100 Years From 1914 To 2019

Our Revered Grand Father District Judge Lahore - Rai Sahib Dina Nath Khanna – 1914

Our Revered Grand Mother Rikhey Deviji with our parents - 1936

Our Revered Father the Late Mr. Justice Prem Nath Khanna who being a Leading senior advocate in civil and corporate affairs was elevated to the Bench of the Delhi High Court 1969 - 1974 which he honorably accepted

Our Revered Mother The Late Mrs. Sushila Khanna

Ravi - Ravinder Nath Khanna
as a boy scout in Mussoorie - 1948

Anil, Ashok, Rama & Ravi - 1956

Ravi - RNK in RP Hall Tennis Team
IIT Kharagpur - 1959

Rama, Uma, Ravi & Anju - 1959

Ravi - RNK sitting fourth from left as the Secretary General of Electrical Engineering Association at IIT-Kharagpur, 1961 with Prof. Menon, Head of the Department & Prof. Roy Chowdhury & other Office Bearers and students of Electrical Engg.

Ravi - RNK on board the Lloyd Triestino Victoria from Mumbai to Napoli - Genoa - Dusseldorf - enroute M & J, Wuppertal, Germany with an inadvertent but distinct victory sign already on way to acquiring knowledge & experience to accomplish a Dream - November 1962

Sitting (L-R): Dipl. Ing. Manfred Schmidt, Frl. Donath, RNK's Boss Dr. Kattner, Frl. Oberhoff, Ing. Wolfgang, Frau Renate Standing (L-R): Frl. Shlikowai, Frl. Kohl, Fri. Schmidt, Frl. Margret, Dr. Franzel, Dipl. Ing. Rohode, Ing Klaus Standing Last Row (L-R): Dipl. Ing. R.N. Khanna, Dipl. Ing. Koening Celebrating my 24th Birthday with Colleagues in my office at Metzenauer & Jung, Wuppertal 1964

RNK with Colleagues and visitors -1965

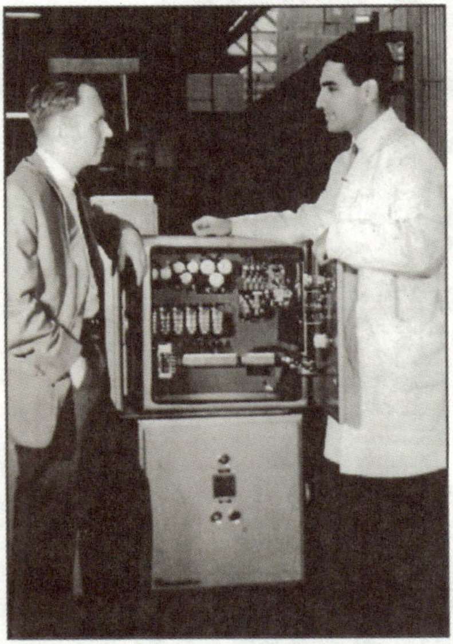

RNK as a Design Engineer at Metzenauer & Jung, Wuppertal - 1962 With Dipe. Ing Rohde with the first Control Panel he designed manufactured and tested all with his own hands

RNK at home at Wuppertal 1963

RNK Skiing in Garmich-1964

RNK in Berlin -1965

The Sacred Statues of Lord Naraynah, Lakshmi and Ganesha Gifted by our mother on our foundation day in 28/01/1966 with her blessing wishing good luck for the newly founded C&S still adore my office with their blessing today

Our First Factory small scale start-up in the car garage behind at the back of our Father's residence at 25 - Rohtak Road, New Delhi - 1966

RNK welcoming the President of Kenya at our Plant at 222, Okhla Industrial Estate arriving formally in The President of India's 6 Door Mercedes Benz 600 SEL Limousine - 1973

RNK as President of the Okhla Industrial Estate at function to Honour visiting overseas Dignitaries - 1978

AK & RNK with the then Union Minister & Dy. Chairman Planning Commission Mr. Mohan Dharia - 1978

AK, Industries Minister George Fernandes, the then Prime Minister Mr. Morarji Desai & RNK - 1975

At the Tikka Ceremony duly blessed by Beeji, Tayeeji, Tayaji, Nanaji, Papa Ji & Bauji on the 11th December 1967 morning

Ravi at Ooty Lake December 16th 1967

Kanwal at Ooty Lake December 16th 1967

Ladies First, Happily and Gracefully honouring the good old tradition without the fuss young men make at most Weddings today as also **Elders First** have stood me well all my life - certainly worth trying - Young Readers!

Refreshing with coconuts at Periyar Lake on way from Ooty to kodaikanal, December - 1967

Ravi & Kanwal

Our Wedding Reception on 12th Dec 1967
Sitting - Raki - Ashok - Anil
Beeji, Masarji, Kanwal, Ravi, Papaji, Massiji
Standing - Subhash, Rama, Sati, Reeti, Joginder, Uma.

Sitting Reeti, Rama, Kanwal, Uma
Standing Sati, Subhash, Ravi, Joginderji

Ravi & Kanwal On the way to Rohtang Pass from Manali - 1971

At Khilanmarg Kashmir with Radhika, Rishi-1981.

The brothers Ravi and Ashok - Chairman and Vice Chairman of C&S Electric, the IITians from Kharagpur (Electrical Engineering Hons 1962) & IIT Madras (Mechanical Engineering 1967). Both have been honored with the rare distinguished Alumni Awards from the respective IITs.

Ravi and Ashok with sons Rishi Nath Khanna and Anuj Khanna, both highly competent Electrical and Electronic Engineers and MBAs from UCLA California & Stern School of Business New York University respectively, being the current illustrious MDs of C&S Electric Limited.

The MDs Anuj, Aditya, Rishi with their sister & Director Radhika

I Have A Dream
I Have A Dream

A song to sing
To help me cope with anything
If you see the wonder of a fairy tale
You can take the future even if you fail

I believe in angels
Something good in everything I see
I believe in angels
When I know the time is right for me
I'll cross the stream - I have a dream

I have a dream, a fantasy
To help me through reality
And my destination makes it worth the while
Pushing through the darkness still another mile
I believe in angels
Something good in everything I see
I believe in angels
When I know the time is right for me
I'll cross the stream - I have a dream
I'll cross the stream - I have a dream

We have a dream, a song to sing
To help me cope with anything
If you see the wonder of a fairy tale
You can take the future even if you fail
We believe in angels
Something good in everything We see
We believe in angels
When we know the time is right for us
We'll cross the stream - We have a dream
We'll cross the stream - We have a dream

We Have A Dream
We Have A Dream

Our First Factory in 1972 at 222, Okhla Industrial Estate III, New Delhi which is now the Head Office of our C&S Electric Ltd.

C&S TC Plant at Noida - 1985

C&S Himoinsa Plant at Rudrapur - 2007

C&S TC II Plant at Noida - 1978

C&S Protection & Measurement Device Plant at Noida - 1984

C&S Switchboard Plant 1 at Noida - 1984

C&S Bus Duct Plant 1 at Greater Noida, Kasna - 1999

C&S Lighting Division Plant at (SIDCUL), Haridwar -2012

C&S Bus Trunking Plant at (SIDCUL), Haridwar - 2001

C&S Export Processing Plant at NSEZ, Noida -2006

C&S Switchboard Plant II at (SIDCUL), Haridwar - 2010

C&S Bus Duct Plant II at (SIDCUL), Haridwar - 2004

C&S MCB Plant at (SIDCUL), Haridwar - 2009

C&S MV Switchgear Plant at Greater Noida

C&S Switchgear Plant at Nantong, China

C&S Eta-com Plant at Boom, Belgium - 2009

C&S Bus Trunking Plant at (SIDCUL), Haridwar

C&S Himoinsa DG Set Plant at Rudrapur

C&S Himoinsa DG Set Plant at Rudrapur -2006

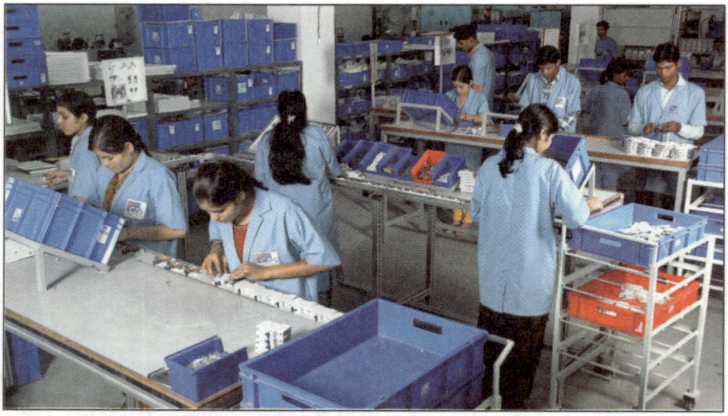

C&S MCB Plant at (SIDCUL), Haridwar-2002

C&S MCB Plant at (SIDCUL), Haridwar-2012

C&S Surface Treatment & Painting Bus Trunking Plant at (SIDCUL), Haridwar - 2002

C&S Sheet Metal Processing Plant at (SIDCUL), Haridwar -2001

One of our R&D Labs at Plant Noida I 1985
GOI approved Research & Development Lab now

C&S Air Circuit Breaker Manufacture & Assembly Plant at Noida

C&S Medium Voltage Switchgear Plant at Greater Noida 2008

C&S Busduct plant at Greater Noida and the larger plant in Haridwar, together with our Bustrunking plant in Both Belgium make us Today The Largest busbar manufacturer in the world.

C&S Switchgear & Switch Fuse Unit Manufacturing at Noida

C&S Moulding Plant TCII at Noida

C&S Air Circuit Breaker Assembly & Testing Plant at Noida

Chapter 4

My Cherished Memories - The Story of My Life & Our Company The C&S Electric Ltd Today as covered by me on our 50th Anniversary 28th January 1966 to 28 January 2016

It almost feels like viewing through a kaleidoscope my challenging life span leading to a unique, beautiful and real life story of a step by step accomplishment in a lifetime.

A cherished childhood dream turning into a vision, after four years of IIT Kharagpur and three years at FANAL, GERMANY. A vision which was finally parked, planted and nurtured in the car garage of my father's residence 50 years ago on the 28th of January 1966 with the blessings of my Rev. Parents and the Lord Almighty.

As I walk down my memory lane today, 50 long & nostalgic years and much more unfolds in front of my eyes. Years that were full of challenges, dreams, desires, directions and commitment. Years that were full of ups and downs, successes, challenges and victories all over again.

Backed by relentless efforts and all out contributions of our highly competent team I have been able to raise over the past 50 rigorous years, supported by my immediate family members, my darling wife Kanwal, my dearest younger brother Ashok and later our illustrious children Rishi, Anuj, Aditya and Radhika and our larger extended family comprising of our most illustrious staff and workmen; our Garage start-up of 1966 occupies a prestigious position among the world leaders in electrical industry today.

Our C&S Electric today is one of India's largest manufacturers of world class Electrical Equipment for Power Generation, Transmission, Distribution, Protection and Automation for the ever growing home & world markets, being India's largest exporter of such products to 85 countries around the globe.

Born and brought up amid the traditions and values of the family comprising my revered grandfather, who was a highly esteemed former District Judge of Lahore–Rai Sahib Dina Nath Khanna and my father the Hon'ble Mr. Justice Prem Nath Khanna, (who was then a young practicing civil Lawyer) my tryst with destiny started at a rather early age of 7 years and 7 months.

It was at midnight of the 22nd August 1947 hardly a week after the partition of India when, in order to save our lives from the rioting and destructive mobs our family was compelled to flee from our ancestral Haveli in Lahore to New Delhi by a chartered Dakota flight leaving all our possessions behind. We were under the kind protection of the brave RSS Volunteers who used to hold a Shakha in the lawns of our Haveli and also of the brave Gorkha army men who helped us with their army jeeps to reach the Lahore Airport safe and sound at midnight.

Life had to be started all over again taking temporary shelter and refuge in my Nanaji's (maternal grandfather) mountain retreat – The Spring Villa in Mussoorie Hills, where he was fortunately holidaying with the rest of the large family.

Despite all the adversities in face of our sudden and complete uprooting, the only redeeming factor during the next few months was indeed the opportunity of spending some quality time with our revered parents and grand-parents.

The great man Dale Carnegie's Books that our father wisely chose to read out to us every morning coupled with the daily Ramayana & the Gita Path at Spring Villa which our Mother and our Nanaji motivated us to attend at Satsangs every evening helped us immensely in inculcating some traditional values in our impressionable years.

Nostalgically, I recall how in the face of challenging situations and compulsions, learnings from my parents and elders inspired me. There was a constant churning of new and emerging thoughts and dreams in my young mind. This led me to take simple, small but bold decisions and steps in my life which I thought would enable our family to rise again and quickly enough after having lost everything during the partition of India.

The 1st Difficult "Bold Decision" to satisfy the fire burning inside me

The 1st difficult bold decision of my life at a very early age was to abandon the age old family tradition and profession of law and judiciary and to try instead to become an engineer and an industrialist one day. I decided to meet and benefit rapidly from the growing needs and opportunities of our vast country after the independence of India in 1947 with an economy struggling for survival.

The young blood in me was yearning to do something more exciting, something new, fresh and scientific–not knowing however exactly what where or how.

There was a fire burning inside me – a passion to do something to make a U-turn towards prosperity even more than what I had seen before.

I could not be subdued by mere circumstances, I could not surrender to mere fate – I will rise, I will have to, I used to think.

The 2nd "Tough Decision" – To do away with my home comforts

The 2nd "Tough Decision" of my life therefore, which I took at the early age of 16 in the year 1956 after my Higher Secondary, was to do away with the comforts of home in Delhi. I had joined and attended the nearby Hindu College at the Delhi University for 3 months only. Here I was offered Botany & Zoology for my B.Sc which was not in line with my pursuit for a career in Engineering.

I therefore boldly choose to proceed instead for more exposure outside home and for my B.Sc. in Physics, Chemistry, Maths to study and stay at the Hostel of the much Renowned Govt. College Ludhiana. There I also got a wonderful opportunity to learn Public Speaking, Tennis, Cricket, Hockey & Swimming etc. which came about most useful in later years of my life.

In May 1958 during my second year of studying for B.Sc Maths, Physics, Chemistry I was fortunate to qualify the challenging IIT Entrance Examination.

Qualifying For The Challenging IIT Kharagpur Entrance Exam

Even back then it was a great honour to be selected amongst hardly 300 students from all over India out of thousands of others who also appeared and attempted in those days to join the one and only IIT-Kharagpur in India.

By June 1962 after a 4-year B. Tech course, after 11 years of schooling and another year of BSc I was fortunate and thrilled to graduate with a 1st Class Hons. Degree in Electrical Engineering from the prestigious IIT- Kharagpur.

The 3rd Most Important Decision of my Life – Learning The German Language Additionally

The 3rd voluntary and 'very tough decision' of my life was that in addition to the extremely heavy load of the final year subjects of B. Tech Hons, I decided nevertheless to take up the additional charge to learn German language as an optional additional subject at IIT-Kharagpur itself.

This paid a rich dividend in my selection in early February 1962 by the Deutscher Akademischer Austausch Dienst (DAAD) of the German Embassy in New Delhi to secure a German Visa and a small DM 250 per month stipend–with a designated six months practical training at Metzenauer & Jung, Wuppertal, Germany. It was one of Germany's major Switchgear and Control Gear manufacturing Company in Low and Medium Voltage sector up to 11 kV.

My thorough and intensive German practical training not only clarified all gaps and barriers in the theoretical knowledge I had gained at IIT-Kharagpur but it also changed the course of the rest of my life and that of my family.

By December 1962 after the first three months of my intensive shop floor training, my Boss at M&J appreciated my grasping ability duly backed by my IIT education from India and decided to absorb me at once as the Design Engineer at their large manufacturing plant at Wuppertal. This was my first great feeling of thrill and victory in my new career. For the first time in my life, I had started thoroughly understanding, appreciating and enjoying my professional work with utmost clarity and an equally great job satisfaction.

Within the next two years, as a young Design & Project Engineer, I travelled on business alone and also with my Boss Dr. Kattner to various customers and M&J Agents throughout Europe and England and gained more and more confidence and experience.

The Amazing Germans

It was a fact that after the WWII the whole of Germany was almost in ashes. German population had to bear the burns of being rejected and deserted by all the other countries of European league. They had lost so much but the will to surge again – and that is all what it takes to resurface.

The Germans had proved themselves tough survivors with an iron will. They had risen from the ashes like a colossus in the field of science and technology within a very short span. Being singled out and completely ruined and yet within no time they had re-established themselves as a formidable European nation in post – World War era.

What worked for them? It wasn't sheer chance that made their resurgence possible. I do not propose to believe in phrases like 'sheer luck' or 'brazen chance'.

The Germans were already advanced in industrial technologies which the entire world was following. While preserving, enriching and implementing those technologies the industrious Germans started Standardization through DIN norms – thus optimizing their efficiency as also the quality of their products to a level better than anywhere else in the World.

Resultantly within no time their backyard Garage units and resurrected factories grew into sizeable industrial institutions.

It was exemplary how courage and positive attitude had led them to amazing success even in their new start-ups. The laborious Germans had showed the world the power of constructive thinking and how blood and sweat and standardized working more than anything else are necessary to attain your goals in all kinds of Industries and other commercial establishments.

A LOT TO LEARN FROM THE GREAT GERMANS

Of course I could anything but admire them on each and every instance of their extraordinary feats! There was a lot to learn from them in each and every field of activity and behaviour in Life.

For instance, I was thrilled and surprised to learn that they even had a simple but most useful Code of Conduct for all residents in a residential colony–even in small villages all over Germany. I may not recall and mention all the codes but noteworthy for my Readers are the following simple ones -

1) Every Saturday Morning the eldest child of each German family would clean the immediate road outside their houses.

2) Also clean the letter box or any litter box externally to keep the surroundings clean.

3) No noisy lawn mowers were permitted for use in gardens to contain noise pollution for the neighbour's sake on all Sundays.

Without remembering and going any further you can well imagine their great collective effort which made Germany in my eyes much cleaner and far better maintained as a Country than all the other neighbouring European Countries including France, Italy, Spain and the UK. This was then accomplished by them almost like the recent 'Swach Bharat' Movement started by our own Worthy Prime Minister Sh Narendra Modi in India.

Besides learning Technical subjects and Business Management

through Part Time Courses in Wuppertal I also fondly enjoyed learning Ballroom Dancing and Western Music through weekend classes. This was a norm for most young Germans in those days and I found it extremely beneficial, relaxing and usable throughout my own life later.

It has been a practice which my dear wife Kanwal also participates in and appreciates very much. It may not be out of place to mention that in the May Queen Ball Annually held in those days at the Oberoi Hotel, New Delhi it was perhaps in 1975 that we as a couple won the First Prize. Among the several gifts we got there was also a three day long free stay at the Ram Bagh Palace in Jaipur which we thoroughly enjoyed in those early days.

My First Overseas Experience in Setting up of a Factory in England.

By mid-1964, owing to my good grasp of product lines and my fluent German besides my excellent English, I was chosen by my German employers to lead a team with three non-English speaking German foremen to England for setting up a new Control Panel and Motor Starter Design & Manufacturing plant with Charles Simmons Controls & Switchboards Sutton Ltd. These were their British partners at Banstead near Wimbledon, Surrey, England. I completed this assignment successfully in eight months. This assignment taught me a lot and I developed a lot of confidence in dealing with new situations and new people at different levels and ages.

How Year after Year I attended and Participated in The Hannover Fair

For three years from 1963 to 1965, I was consecutively chosen & designated at the Stalls of M&J at The Hannover Fair every year. This gave me a further confidence in dealing with their vast Product & Project Lines and also with several overseas customers and engineers including Indian Industrialists who regularly visited the Hannover Fair.

Besides I got a wonderful exposure to the product lines, people and technologies of other large competitors of M&J (now Honeywell) – like Siemens, Klockner Moeller (now Eaton), Telemecanique (now Schneider), Stromberg (now ABB), Mitsubishi, Toshiba, GE and even some Indian companies like Siemens India Ltd, ABB, English Electric, & L&T (now Schneider).

Interesting Appointment Offered In Israel Which I Could Not Accept

Early in 1965, immediately after the Hannover fair, I was offered an assignment to proceed to Israel for replicating what I had done at Banstead, U.K. This offer was however for a three year long assignment at even more attractive terms than the previous assignment in England. If necessary, I was even offered a change to the German Nationality since my Indian passport did not recognize Israel in those days.

As a young man, I was in a strange dilemma. On one hand it was most exciting to accept this challenging offer. On the other hand it amounted to putting in cold storage my good old childhood dream and desire to start an Industry of my own.

After a few months of deep introspection, I saw with clarity the light at the end of my own search tunnel that I had a mission in life to fulfil my own cherished dream of setting up an industry of my own back home in India.

The 4th Most Difficult & Bold Decision of my Life – Resigning From My Promising German Job

The 4th most difficult and bold decision of my life therefore was to resign from my lucrative and well established job at M&J and return to my roots in India by October 1965. I had brought back with me several latest products as samples, designs and technologies for manufacturing world class sophisticated electricals for power generation, distribution, control, protection and automation in India where until then only multinationals used to rule the roost.

Having once been invited by the Indian Embassy in Bonn for a cup of tea with our worthy Former Prime Minister Mr. Jawahar

Lal Nehru in 1963, I was deeply impressed by his Words of Wisdom, which reignited my own dream to start on my own one day. His message sounded something like -

Words Of Wisdom And Inspiration By Our Worthy Prime Minister Mr Jawaharlal Nehru -

"My dear Young men from India – I am thrilled to meet you and to learn how well you are studying, learning and gaining experience in Germany.

Time should soon come for you to come back home to India and with the rich experience you have gained here, start your own Industries to build an India of tomorrow. An India that we can all be proud of.

Today you are participating-in and witnessing a Historical, Astronomical Rise and Growth of the Great German Industry & Economy. This has only been possible through the enormous hard work of the disciplined Germans after a complete destruction of their Industry and the Country during the World War-II.

India likewise beckons you my Dear Young Countrymen to come back home and build your own Industries to serve and build your Country your own INDIA and your own selves.

Jai Hind!

My First Bold and Practical Experiment on the D3 & C Formula

Returning back home to start on my own was my life's first bold, practical and live experiment with the 'D3 & C formula' (Dream, Desire, Direction & Commitment) which I learnt from my learned German Professor Dr. Muller.

However, it was becoming even more exciting now with an absolute clear direction and utmost commitment to my newly founded Controls & Switchgear Company (as it was known back then). It was my own beloved new dream project.

Our Foundation Day and our First Factory in our Garage

On a crisp, bright sunny wintry morning of the 28th of January 1966 which my mother decided was an auspicious day for the family being my father's and my own birthday could also be the birthday of my new Company.

After a brief Pooja Ceremony conducted by my revered Mother following a Havan (ritual), Halwa-Prasad specially prepared and distributed by her lovingly and the auspicious breaking of the Nariyal (Coconut) the Controls & Switchgear Company was finally founded and launched in the Car Garage of our father's residence at 25-Rohtak Road, New Delhi.

The Controls & Switchgear Company as we called ourselves originally, was founded with a tall dream and utmost dedication to bring back to India world class products, systems, equipment and services in the field of power generation, distribution and control – a field which was until then dominated by multinationals despite their older products in India.

The newly white washed and clean little factory in our garage was duly equipped with some components like essential tools, testing jigs and technical Dossiers and Drawings brought back by me from Germany, neatly displayed on the wall cabinets like I had seen in small workshops in Germany. In addition there was my Drawing Board and its' big stand besides my old German Drawing Instruments – all well placed and exhibited.

The wooden crates that brought my tools and tackles from Germany were converted by Amrik Singh a talented carpenter for Rs 150/- only into two sturdy working tables and elementary side boards. Besides there was an old office table and some old chairs which had been gifted by my father.

Hence with hardly Rs 10,000/- to invest still left in my pocket from my German Job earnings, and after buying certain tools & tackles and testing equipment from Germany and accommodating my travel expenses back home, the Operations at our new factory started with utmost enthusiasm. In addition to my own self, only one good Electrician was selected and employed to join as the 1st worker of the Company.

Although on 28th Jan 1966, the foundation of our Controls & Switchgear Company in the car garage of our house may have been very small but the Dream, the Desire, the Direction and the Commitment behind this was indeed BIG and utmost from day one.

Most Indian customers of M&J Germany from the Machine-Tools, Paper, Lifts and Cranes and Sugar Industries with whom I had been dealing earlier were approached. They appreciated my new indigenous endeavour and were motivated to place trial orders on us.

Drawing strength from the slogan 'Lack of Resources makes you more Resourceful', I approached Siemens Delhi for essential Control Gear components on 30 days credit terms. Other small workshops around who could fabricate and supply sheet metal parts to our specific designs also pitched in. All design, assembly, wiring and testing & quality control work was however, done in house under my own supervision before I could train more people to conform to our quality expectations according to the German quality standards, workmanship and after sales service like I had myself learnt and imbibed at M&J.

Not only were our new customers pleasantly surprised and completely satisfied with the excellent quality of our products, they greatly appreciated being additionally supported by our design services for their new products in addition to the after sales services like the installation, testing and commissioning assistance which I personally provided free of cost through my own regular visits to their plants and factories.

Such personalized customer service undoubtedly led to winning more and more orders in due course. For the first time in my life, I clearly started appreciating and practicing Dr. Metzenauer and Dr. Kattner's words 'Customer is the King' & 'Small & Only Small Steps lead to Perfection but Perfection is not a small thing etc.'

To my great surprise and satisfaction, within the first 12 months we were flooded with repeat small orders from our highly satisfied customers. Even the Senior Managers of Siemens

India and English Electric, who were personally known to me from the Hannover Fair, visited our small factory before agreeing to give credit to us and were pleasantly surprised to see the excellent quality of our products and our neat systematic designs and manufacturing set up. Resultantly, they also started placing orders for small and urgent jobs which we executed to their complete satisfaction.

With my bare minimum overheads, the net profit after taxes was pumped back into the business which enabled purchase of our 1st Ambassador Car and some additional tools and tackles by the end of the very first fiscal year and more so with the passage of time.

As the business expanded, the unused and almost 400 sq. mts. of cleanly paved courtyard within our house in front of the car garage became very handy before we shifted to our newly constructed and well equipped 40,000 sq ft Manufacturing Plant at 222-Okhla Industrial Estate in 1972 on the lines and style I had experienced in Germany.

How The Family Strength is Cultivated

My younger brother Ashok is motivated to join me

I always loved to share my own learnings with my loving and illustrious younger brother Ashok and motivated him to join me immediately after his B. Tech in Mechanical Engineering from IIT-Madras. I apprised him and shared all my learnings so that he could also reinforce and share my vision for the future of our Company. Ashok has always had a very special position in my life. Therefore, after Ashok joined our foundation became even stronger.

Ashok and I never looked behind and as Brothers we forged our energies together to strengthen **C&S** our Beloved Venture which according to IEEMA, PHDCCI, FICCI, COSMA and the Book "Thought Leaders" by Tata McGraw Hills and many others has been cited as one of the most inspiring sagas of our time after the independence of India.

Over the years, we have worked relentlessly in pursuit of

this objective and world leaders who shared our passion for quality and manufacturing competence in India have come forward to join hands with us in technical collaborations and joint ventures with buy back arrangements, such as – Simelectro France, Terasaki Japan, Stromberg ABB-Finland, Telemecanique-France, AVK-SEG, Germany Leroy Somer-France, Wago-Germany, Gewiss, Italy, Efacec-Portugal and several others.

Shifting our operations to our brand new Manufacturing Plant at 222, Okhla Industrial Estate, Phase III, New Delhi

Since 25, Rohtak Road, from where we were operating our small scale industry was a residential area, we were originally offered a 1000 square yard plot of land at Naraina.

I explained our project in detail to the Director of Industries who finally appreciated our genuine demand and allotted a 2500 Sq. yards plot instead, at the auspicious number 222 in the prestigious Okhla Industrial Estate Phase III.

A requisite loan of Rs. 6.50 Lakhs was sanctioned by the Delhi Financial Corporation. Soon one of the best of its time and a most modern 40000 Sq feet Factory Plant close to the German Designs and complete with a basement as I had experienced in Germany was built by. All requisite Machinery was also installed for Fabrication and Surface Treatment besides all the Testing and Measuring Equipment we needed. The loan was paid back with interest well within the prescribed limits of time to absolute satisfaction of the lenders.

New Product Launches

Year after year, after **C&S** launched our successful Make in India Drive by introducing one after the other the World's latest Products and Designs with minor changes made suitable for the Indian Environment and the Indian Market, most other world leaders (like Siemens, ABB, L&T, English Electric who were already in the Indian Market) were also motivated to change their older products in India. They did so by bringing their own latest lines to the gain of the Indian Market and

Indian customers. For us, the gain was two folds since such latest products also opened doors for us in new markets overseas where we are the largest exporters from India today.

The Electrical Manufacturing Industry and Trade in India well recognizes how we have led a 50 year long and successful mission that has brought respect and recognition to the Make in India Label worldwide and has become a legend today.

Today, we can say with pride that as brothers Ashok and I have worked together and enjoyed an excellent fraternity full of love, trust and mutual respect and regard. No wonder on the horizon of the Indian family business partnerships, our success together over the last 50 years has undoubtedly created exemplary impression outside as also for our own posterity to appreciate, emulate and further strengthen in the times to come.

"The C&S Electric Group" as we are called today, is a vision which took off from a car garage in the backyard of our father's house. It has since become a 'Garage to Globe' legend today, stretching across 17 world-class manufacturing plants including a prestigious acquisition of a unique Bus Duct Manufacturing Plant in Belgium and setting up of a Green Field Switchgear and Control Gear Manufacturing Plant in China with Distributors in 84 countries.

Today we have a motivated team of nearly 5000 people including 1000 engineers, professionals & technocrats manufacturing sophisticated High-tech World Class products for Thermal, Hydro, Nuclear and Solar power generation, distribution, control, protection and automation, not only for the growing Indian market where we share business on equal footing with large multinationals today but also for being India's largest exporters successfully exporting our products regularly to 84 countries around the globe.

Some of our products are regularly branded or being regularly used by world leaders like General Electric-USA, Eaton-USA, CEFCO, US and Canada Alstom-France, ABB-Europe, Finland, Cromptons and MEM-UK, Mitsubishi-Japan and Phillips and

Panasonic-India among others.

With a sturdy foundation of 50 long years of engineering excellence, the C&S Electric Ltd today is surging ahead towards an even more exciting next phase of growth and consolidations in the years to come. C&S Electric's growth over the years has been synchronous with achieving complete self-sufficiency in indigenous design and manufacture of a full range of world class Electricals for the Power Generation, Distribution, Transmission and Protection sectors with Voltage up to 33 KV.

Today we are an Integrated Electrical Equipment Manufacturer of world class Products & Services widely used in India, with a large global footprint. We are exporting regularly to 85 Countries around the globe besides manufacturing and branding several products for other world leaders. Our vast and unique product range has already carved out a special niche for us amongst only a counted few industries and world leaders who do likewise and more.

The high level of quality and reliability factor of C&S Products and Services is due to our dedicated and meticulous approach and adherence to International standards and quality norms in all our product ranges by acquiring some of the world's most outstanding technologies, diligently assimilating them and developing them further to adopt for growing and challenging requirements of power networks in India and around the world.

You are all aware that from day one our Company has never compromised on quality. We have over the years invested intensively in training our people in the best cutting edge management and manufacturing systems such as Six Sigma, 5S, TPM, Kaizen and TQC which has added to a huge sense of ownership in our employees at all levels.

Surging ahead from an enlightened past to an even more promising future

World leaders in the Electrical Technology who recognized our manufacturing and marketing competence and who shared our passion for quality and the enormous growth of the Indian markets and economy, have come forward one by one to join hands with us in the form of Technical Collaborations and Joint Ventures with buy back arrangements over the last 5 decades.

Although many of our Collaborations & Joint Ventures have already lapsed the agreed durations, C&S has always expressed its utmost appreciation and gratitude to all its former Technology Partners and readily offers to them it's Make in India world class Manufacturing Services & Products which are increasingly becoming more cost competitive and attractive worldwide today.

Owing to our vast reservoir of Technical knowhow and Manufacturing expertise gained, maintained and enhanced further in-house over the last 50-years, four of our Manufacturing Plants have already acquired the unique status of Govt. of India's approved Research & Development Centres with inbuilt testing facilities where renowned international Test-Centres and Laboratories like the UL and others examine, verify and witness testing of products before certifying and approving them to conform to various standards.

The future is full of exciting opportunities. We at C&S Electric are fully geared up–to undertake new business opportunities by expanding our offerings and enhancing our competitiveness, by maximizing the utilization of our existing infrastructure and enhancing it as and when necessary.

Besides our unique and outstanding Product Range, our greatest strength today is our vast reservoir of technical know-how and manufacturing competence & facilities coupled further with our highly skilled and committed work force who have been the cornerstone of our continuing journey ensuring success in all our endeavours.

On this auspicious occasion My Dear Colleagues, let truth and wisdom lead us to our firm belief that our success over the last 50 years has been a journey we must continue hand in hand, step by step and is not a destination where we can stop as a dedicated team committed to excellence.

Let us charge ourselves and our batteries once again today.

Let us demonstrate our commitment to ourselves and our beloved company, to our valued customers in India and around the world for decades and generations to come ahead.

by recalling and citing with pleasure in one loud and thundering voice together our well proven and sacred in-house Company Mantra once again today.

We Can Do It – We Shall Do It – We Will Do It

Chapter 5

Chronological Details Of The Step By Step Growth Of Our C&S Electric Ltd

From The Foundation Year 1966 to the year 2012

Chronological Details Of The Step By Step Growth Of Our C&S Electric Ltd

From The Foundation Year 1966 To The Year 2012

OUR OPERATIONS START IN THE GARAGE OF MY FATHER'S HOUSE

TO BUILD SWITCHGEAR & SEQUENTIAL SWITCHING CONTROL PANELS FOR CRANES, MACHINE TOOLS, SUGAR MILLS, STEEL PLANTS & INDUSTRY IN GENERAL

The freshly white washed garage factory with make shift side-boards, two working tables and stools, an old office desk and three chairs plus of course my drawing board. A display of tools and tackles, catalogues aligned neatly on the walls–it was almost like what I had seen in the small German factories.

Beautiful sandal-wood statues of Lord Ganesha, Maa (Goddess Mother) Lakshmi and Lord Vishnu gifted by my Revered Mother were placed on the little shelf behind my table.

These sacred statues with the blessings of my Revered Parents (Beejee and Papajee) as we called them fondly, still adore my office on the side-board overlooking my working desk–reminding me of them as I bow my head in salutations every morning when I enter my office.

Nariyal or the auspicious coconuts, two of them were broken (a ritual) on the gate of the garage by Papaji and me. Halwa Prasad was given to us by my Beeji (mother) after a small Pooja and Aarti she performed to invoke the blessings of the Lord to supplement my hard work and labour in establishing our then small, Controls & Switchgear Company.

The knowledge of drawings, designing and building Control Panels for the previously mentioned Industries was still fresh in my mind.

Some of my former customers at the German Company whom I used to serve in Germany, when approached sincerely were kind enough to be convinced to take the risk of ordering their Control Panels on me at least for trial.

I bought most vital electrical components from Siemens. The sheet-metal job was done to my own designs and precision through a small but quality conscious sheet-metal workshop in Panchkuin Road, New Delhi, which was owned by a rare quality conscious technician Mr Makhan Singh. I go my first Panels painted after proper Surface Treatment and Passivation from the local automobile repair units and started assembling wiring and testing of intricate Control Panels in my own garage factory. I handled things with my own hands under my own supervision using one and only one electrician I could afford to start with back then.

Within a month my first experiments had succeeded before the end of February 1966. The first Control Panel I had delivered to my own Brother-in-law Sh. Joginderji (for my sister Uma's Company). My first deal met with flawless success. It was soon followed by repeat orders from them and from several of my new customers who were thrilled to find me as a convenient local source who could also help them freely in Designing and Automation of their machinery enhancing their performance and durability.

Soon I contacted several other Manufacturing Units who were earlier importing Control Panels from my German Employers overseas or those who were buying them from the heavily loaded Siemens or L&T in India with their plants in Bombay. Buying equally good quality Panels from me with the full back up of after-sales service at competitive rates and assured quick delivery were indeed my USPs Soon my own customers became my marketing strength and our reputation spread around.

UTMOST CARE FOR QUALITY FROM DAY-ONE

Utmost care in quality, design and workmanship, well learnt in Germany and practiced in my new workshop from day one stood me well. My first year's turnover was hardly one lakh rupees but the profit was phenomenal. My overheads being at home were bare minimum. My customers were very, very happy. By now I had used my father's car and driver on very rare occasions and mostly used Scooter Rikshaws for travel.

In the 2nd year, we turned out goods worth Rs 5.80 lakhs with an equal ratio in profits. My 2nd year's profit could sustain to buy me a brand new Ambassador Car to carry on my marketing operations. Besides, a few essential basic Machines for good Fabrication, Surface Treatment and Spray Painting etc. were bought and introduced at my garage factory. Some of them were installed in the open court yard at the backyard of the house compound in front of my garage. The strength of workmen and employees had meanwhile risen to eleven.

Relationship With Siemens India Grows

Most of the vital Control Gear components I had bought from Siemens. Their New Delhi Branch Head Mr. Om Parkash and Manager Mr. Talwani had visited my small scale factory and were thrilled to see the quality work I was carrying out. Their General Manager Mr. Sidhu was my senior from IIT Kharagpur and was most thrilled to see my progress. Moreover he was most satisfied to observe that my PDCs (postdated cheques), which was the mode of payments in those days always encashed readily and were paid on due dates without any failure even once. Our relationship with Siemens grew with leaps and bounds as they also started placing orders on us for quicker deliveries.

I was able to indigenize within the first three years, two vital components namely Line-up Terminal Block used in Control Panels and also Control & Signaling Push Buttons & Pilot Lamps – similar in quality almost to M&J the German company I used to work with.

Small Moulding Machines were also installed within my house-cum-factory and at the end of our 3rd year we were a team of almost 30 people determined to accelerate growth.

1. WINNING OF PRESTIGIOUS MARINE SWITCHGEAR CONTRACT AGAINST BIG GIANTS LIKE SIEMENS, L&T, ENGLISH ELECTRIC & GEC

My desire to become an exclusive Manufacturer in some areas of Technology where we did not have to depend on the components from multinationals like Siemens, L&T, English Electric and others was always there.

Consequently, I dared to quote for an advertised tender for the first ever indigenization of complete electricals for the first three Leander Class Frigate Warships to be built by the Indian Navy at the Mazagon Docks, Mumbai. For this project all the components were to be specially designed, developed and manufactured in India to withstand shock and vibration to the extent of 60g and water proof under 25 meter head of water.

Competing directly with giants like Siemens, English Electric, L&T and GEC and with a team of hardly 30 something people at my command plus a rather meager collection of machines to produce intricate Control Panels, Junction Boxes and specialized Light Fittings etc. for India's first indigenous warships, I observed nevertheless to grab this good opportunity and dared to compete with the large multinational houses for the first time.

During six months of negotiations with the Indian Navy for indigenization of all the electricals for the first Leander Class Frigate to be built in India, I had taken the risk of indigenizing more than half a dozen of items and subjected them to vigorous testing. I procured approval from National Defence Laboratories to withstand shock and vibration to the extent of 60g as also for the environmental protection under 25 meters head of seawater etc. This was never done by any of my large multinational friends and competitors.

Resultantly, the price negotiating committee of the Ministry of Defence told us that though they could not ignore our offer since it was the lowest in value with certain test reports also in our favour, but they were not certain whether we could ultimately produce these goods and supply them in time and the quantity needed.

We met Mr. M.M. Sen the Defence Secretary and explained to him how under the personal encouragement and assurances of the former Prime Minister of India Mr. Jawahar Lal Nehru during his visit to Bonn a few years ago he had called Indian students to the Indian Embassy for a get-together and had assured them that 'their place of work was back home bringing back the benefit of their knowledge and experience' gained overseas.

We explained to them, that a Germany trained IITian had come back home to India to set up a home Industry which already manufactured these products and tested them to the specifications. Besides I had quoted the lowest price, then why were we not worthy of the order?

Gradually, after visiting our Factory, the Navy officials were convinced of our capabilities and they were bold enough to place the entire order on us worth almost Rs 35 lakhs. This was a very large value single order even for the big multinationals in those days. Besides, it carried an advance of 20% i.e. appx. Rs 5 lakhs as development charges.

As a matter of fact, the State Bank of India had to make exceptions in their procedure because the Bank Guarantee which the Magazon Docks wanted for the Rs 5 lakhs advance payment for development charges, could not be given by the State Bank of India. It was so since till that date we did not have any collateral property in our own name whatsoever to mortgage the same in favour of the Bank.

Moreover, I had made up my mind not to ask my father for any financial assistance or counter guarantee whatsoever, since I appreciated that he had a lot already on his shoulders to settle and get his six children married.

The State Bank of India Secretary and Treasurer Mr Sarkar in New Delhi who was a keen admirer of our spirit to sustain, after a great deal of persuasion finally appreciated my position and came forward to give us the bank guarantee. This was however on the assurance that the Bank's 25% margin will nevertheless be recovered from the proceeds of the advance and that's how things started to move ahead.

Complete and resounding ultimate success was achieved in designing, manufacturing and delivery for the above order on time. This success lead to repeat orders from Navy for different products. Consequently almost two decades later, the Indian Navy trusted our Company being a 100% Indian Company for indigenizing the Complete Shock Hardened Switchgear to 600g shock vibrations for use in the most prestigious first Nuclear Submarine Project that was to be produced in India.

2. OUR DIVERSIFICATION INTO ELECTRONIC ROAD TRAFFIC SIGNALS

Having succeeded in securing the Defence Naval jobs and executing them successfully, the desire within me to do something even more exclusive which other multinationals with higher resources were not doing, was very much and always there.

In those days, Road Traffic Signals were nowhere to be seen in India except the one and only one on Rajpath, India Gate in New Delhi. Some clumsy looking Control Boxes had been rested on wooden tables by the National Physical Laboratory using Electronic Vacuum Tube Switching System. This worked for a few hours and failed thereafter until the on duty Policeman went and gave it a few hard kicks with his tough boots. The equipment and the installation looked really pathetic and clumsy to a qualified engineer like me who was used to well-designed robust systems.

By this time we had our modern and well equipped state of the art factory in Okhla which was very well laid out – just like small German Plants. Besides, we had already acquired our own new and proper Shearing, Bending and Welding Machines to accomplish Sheet-Metal, cutting, slotting, bending and welding to requisite perfection by then. We had made our own

Surface Treatment Plant and Painting and Stoving Plants as also our Electrical and Electronic Test Equipment Labs to test whatever we produced.

We therefore, assumed and took upon ourselves the task, the challenge and the courage to build India's first properly designed Road Traffic Signals.

We made full use of our knowledge to manufacture Control Panels, Electronic Sequential Switching Controls with Transistorized Devices custom designed, developed and tested by us. Properly fitted contactors were wired and robustly soldered through special terminals to the electronic systems and PCBs through numbered line up Terminal Blocks as in modern Control Panels.

The whole thing was professionally designed and housed in water tight outdoor type Feeder Pillars. The underground cables supplied power to our own specially designed Traffic Signal Lanterns mounted on properly designed Traffic Signal Poles with Terminal Blocks for ease in connecting and disconnecting whenever necessary.

The whole thing was well conceived and exclusively designed and manufactured by us for the first time in India. Till today, our products are working successfully in all parts of the country.

We also designed and built world class Synchronized Traffic Signals to promote free flow of traffic at the India Gate Hexagon, New Delhi. Soon all the most prominent areas in the National Capital and other big cities had our Traffic Signals working to complete satisfaction. We soon became India's first and the largest manufacturers of world class traffic signals.

The business zoomed and we covered most of the big Indian cities with our products. The only competition came from Indian Telephone Industries Ltd. (ITI) Bangalore, who being a P.S.U. were naturally very high priced. Being a Public Sector organization, however, they were also able to get certain orders using 10% price preference besides their apparent muscle power. We had to bear the burden of the bureaucratic delays in release of payments and connected hardships that we were not used to however.

By now, besides Control Panels which was our prime product earlier, we had started regularly producing Switchgear for the Navy and Traffic Signals for the Municipalities all over India.

ITI-Bangalore Chairman Mr I.K. Gupta despite being our competitors was very much impressed and appreciated our Technical competence and we became good friends since then.

We at C&S also needed good ITI Telephone Relays in our Traffic Signals for switching electronic impulses and imports were not allowed back then. Soon however the ITI stopped giving us the Relays since they were themselves stuck up with large demand of Relays for Telephone Exchanges throughout India which they found very difficult to meet also.

The Need For Know-How From Public Sector

I.T.I. Bangalore For Manufacturing Telephone Relays for Supply Back & Personal Usage

I had persuaded Development Wing of the Industry Ministry to import Telephone Relays for our use in Traffic Signals. They asked us to meet the ITI instead and support their manufacturing strength if we could.

Nothing seemed to be moving with usual bureaucratic delays until one day I saw our famous great Minister Mr. Manubhai Shah at a Bus Stand on Janpath quietly waiting in que for the next bus. I was surprised to see the great man in distress and stopped my car to offer him a lift. He was going to the Teen Murti Lane and incidentally I was also going to my parents' place at H.No.19 Teen Murti Lane.

Mr. Shah enquired who I was and I communicated my introduction. Having been a Former Industry Minister he was keen to see our start up Unit then. He was thrilled to know the excellent progress we were making and was surprised to see how we were rolling out the Country's first Traffic Signals also.

Once he learnt of our bottle-neck with the ITI over Relays

he was kind enough to call Mr. Bahuguna (the then Minister for Communication). Mr. Bahuguna appreciated our desire and capability to assist the ITI in Supplement Relay Supplies and advised me to meet Mr. J K Gupta, The Chairman of ITI Bangalore and explain my problems. The suggested solution was a win-win for both sides.

I soon met the Chairman I.T.I. Bangalore seeking the Technology to manufacture Telephone Relays so that we could supply back to them as well. With great difficulty and initial reluctance they sought DGTDs permission and finally agreed.

We paid them a lump sum fee of Rs 1.25 lakhs they had demanded to share the Technology for Strowger System Electromagnetic Relays in addition to 5% royalty on all we sold back to them or to other Telephone circuits in India.

Consequently we became (inclusive of selling back to them) the exclusive suppliers to them and others of Relays which we manufactured with great proficiency–successfully catering to their demands for the next 15 years besides using them ourselves in our Traffic Signals.

The Competition Hots Up

By the year 1976, after almost ten years of our establishment we had started competing with the likes of Siemens, L&T, English Electric and ABB etc. for large tenders that came from Steel Plants or Power Corporations. However, these multinationals were so wary of our success that they started twisting our tail by denying us the supply of their vital components in time–consequently delaying our supplies to some highly prestigious projects. Such were the usual tactics employed to retain their own exclusivity.

Our Natural Expansion Into Sophisticated Switchgear Products:

Considering the fact that adversity was the mother of invention we tried to give shape to my own one time dream of self-manufacturing high quality Electrical Products and Components like Contactors, Relays, Motor Starters, Switches,

Fuses, Circuit Breakers and Protection Relays etc. These were until then only in the domain of big established multinationals alone who had been functioning in India already for a long time.

In the year 1982, for a large 3 x 250 MW Farakka Thermal Power Plant, the NTPC refused to consider giving specifications to us since we were not manufacturing Contactors, Relays, Switches, Fuses or Circuit Breakers. Their demand was however that Indian manufacturers if any, can only be qualified if they manufacture themselves any one of the above vital Components – the rest could be procured from the other established manufacturers. Time was now ripe for me to convert this adversity into advantage and to bring world class Technologies to India.

Our Pledge To Build World Class Electricals:

My Dear Readers you will be pleased to learn that as an IITian from Kharagpur 1962 batch with almost sixteen years of experience on the Indian horizon till then, I pledged myself to bring the best of Technologies from the world over to India and to produce some of the world's most outstanding Switchgear products – way ahead of the technologies used by other multinationals in India till then.

3. DESIGN & MANUFACTURE OF SEMI & FULLY DRAWOUT MOTOR & POWER CONTROL CENTRES FOR THERMAL, HYDRO AND NUCLEAR POWER PLANTS:

In the early 1980s major players in Power Utilities as like NTPC, Nuclear Power Corporation and the National Hydro Electric Power Body had decided that for the future Power Projects they would only procure Switch Boards that could be of fully withdraw-able type both in Power and in the Auxiliary Systems thereby minimizing the down time whenever necessary.

Having become major suppliers of our fixed type of Switch Boards sharing the market at equal footings with the major multinationals like Siemens, Alstom, ABB, L&T etc. we had two choices–either to withdraw from this field or to indigenously develop such sophisticated systems in-house.

We took up the challenge and specially designed and developed fully withdraw-able jaw clamping Power Terminals as also the Control Terminals at par with the best in the world. We also tested our Switch Boards and got them approved from the Central Power Research Institute in Bhopal. This was a major break-through achievement. Consequently we also started exporting such Switch Boards to various countries around the World.

4. NEW MINIATURE PCB MOUNTED TELEPHONE RELAYS UNDER KNOWHOW FROM ZETTLER-GERMANY 1985-1990

As mentioned in the foregoing summary, by the year 1974 our Company had already started manufacturing Strowger Relays under technical know-how from I.T.I. Bangalore. These Relays we regularly supplied to the I.T.I. for the entire Indian Telephone network besides using them for our own road traffic control systems.

In the early 1980s the I.T.I. gradually changed from Strowger System to the Modern Switching Alcatel System which needed totally different miniature Relays to Alcatel Designs.

We faced this challenge rapidly by getting the know-how from Zettler, Germany who were one of the major manufacturers and suppliers of a full range of Miniature Relays. We further brought minor changes to adapt to Indian conditions and added more sophisticated machinery and testing systems.

Soon thereafter we imported the entire plant from Zettlerl and enhanced our capacity to meet the growing requirements of the New and enlarged Telephone Network.

5. AIR CIRCUIT BREAKERS FROM 630A TO 6300A UNDER TECHNICAL COLLABORATION WITH WORLD FAMOUS TERASAKI OF JAPAN (1982-87) :

Considering the urgency of the NTPC Farakka challenge I traveled to Hannover, Germany and went to the Stalls of each and every renowned manufacturer of Air Circuit Breakers including that of Terasaki of Japan.

Most of them except Terasaki were already present in India one way or the other.

The employees of Terasaki told me that Mr. Yasuhiko Terasaki, the President had left the day before for Glasgow (Scotland) where Terasaki were holding their Annual Sales Meet with their distributors in Europe & England.

I had recognized that Terasaki were one of the world leaders in the field of Air Circuit Breakers. The very next day I with my wife Kanwal traveled from Hannover to Glasgow. We were staying in the same hotel and the most beautiful Golf Resort called Loch Lomond at Hotel Lomond Castle was within the Lane where Mr. Terasaki was staying with their distributors.

We played golf together during the days and to Mr. Terasaki, his General Manager Yamamoto and other colleagues I explained the enormous opportunity knocking at both mine and his doors in India. Mr Terasaki invited me to come over to Japan the next week which I did and at the end of my visit to Osaka, I signed my first agreement of Technical Collaboration with Terasaki of Japan to produce world class Air Circuit Breakers in India – of a quality way ahead of all the multinationals till then in India.

By virtue of this collaboration, we were qualified to quote for the Farakka Tender and won this tender then worth almost Rs.7 crores originally utilizing Terasaki imported components for Air Circuit Breakers assembled in India. Within the next three years however, we started rolling out complete world class Terasaki Air Circuit Breakers from our brand new second Manufacturing Plant in Noida.

Six of our engineers were trained at Japan. Our Circuit Breakers assembled in India together with rest of the Switchgear have stood us well at the Farakka Thermal Power Plant and have been working satisfactorily for more than the last 25 years. Thereafter our C&S Terasaki Circuit Breakers were supplied and utilized in numerous Thermal, Atomic and Hydro Electric Power Plants in India and across the world which bears a clear testimony to the quality of the product that we developed and manufacture.

Today, we supply the largest Circuit Breakers to customers where deliveries from Japan are taking too long. Meanwhile we have also used our own Designs and Development Wing to enhance capacity of the Circuit Breakers which we now export around the world and even Brand–for some well-known Houses in France and in South Africa.

6. CONTACTORS, OVERHEAD RELAYS, MOTOR STARTERS FROM 9A TO 1600A IN JOINT VENTURE WITH TELEMECANIQUE OF FRANCE (1984-2003) :

After the 1982 Collaboration with Terasaki, my mind was now open to venture in the field of sophisticated and largely used Electrical Components and the next product in my list was Contactors, Overload Relays and Motor Starters. I was already very familiar to these sophisticated products from my days with M&J FANAL (1962 to 1965) who were now being taken over by Honeywell of USA.

Since no other manufacturer was prepared to offer the requisite technical know-how, we approached Allen West in the UK who had been taken over by GE and were now called by the name Simplex GE.

Soon we signed a Technical Collaboration Agreement with Simplex GE of U.K. owned by GE of USA which only permitted us the import of components and assembly thereof. However, we realized that the product was a bit too outmoded, bulky and expensive as compared to smaller and newer designs with Siemens and L&T who were the main manufacturers of those products in India then.

The Chairman of Telemecanique-France Mr. Jacques

Walla had been met by me at the Hannover Fair several times.

I met Mr. Jacques Walla again at Hannover and later at their Head Quarters in Paris. He came to the Elecrama Fair and was disappointed to see our Simplex GE Contactors displayed at our Stalls. He was very friendly with me having known me since 1965 in Hannover when he was only a Senior Manager with Telemecanique, and used to explain his products to a young engineer like me even though I came from his German Competitors – FANAL.

He was however enamored by my small company and by the tremendous progress we had made in the field of Electrical Control Panels till then. He used to say 'your company reminds me of how Telemecanique used to be several decades ago at their own start of operations'.

Thereafter, he visited India on two occasions with his own Technical Managers and Directors and expressed his desire to collaborate with us although they had been tied up until then with the house of Kirloskars for over 20 years. He explained to me that Kirloskars were a great Company however they were concentrating more on their mechanical equipment and therefore Telemecanique were looking for a new partner.

In the month of November 1983, I received a letter from Mr. Jacques Walla saying that they were on the wrong foot in India and he would like me to visit with my Managers to France where if the discussions succeed, it could lead to our joint venture.

To my surprise on landing in Paris, I found that two other well-known smaller Indian Companies like us had also been called for discussions and interviews with their team. Out of the league they intended to select and partner with one finally.

With my General Manager (Technical) Mr P.P Singh and my Chartered Accountant Mr Sharma I camped in Paris for next four weeks–from 15th November till 15th December. Finally we raised a toast on French Champagne and signed our first Joint Venture Agreement with Telemecanique of France who were the world leaders in the field of Contactors, Overload Relays, Motor Starters, Push Buttons, Pilot Lamps, Limit Switches and a host of other superior products. All these Telemecanique products were called the 'Rolls Royce' in the market i.e. the ultimate–the best designed and performing products in the world.

For me it was one of my greatest achievements of life! As if an old dream was finally coming true. Our joint venture with Telemecanique France lasted very well from 1983 till the year 2003.

Then we separated amicably. The reason being they had been bought over by the greater and large House of Schneider Electrique, France. Consequently they were keen to export directly from France to India in a big way and we were being prevented to export from India.

We agreed to part as partners and bought over their shares and the company which was until then called Telemecanique & Controls (India) Ltd and then became Controls & Switchgear Contactors Ltd.

In the process, we permitted them to start their own manufacturing in India if they wanted to–on their own and likewise we were also free to export our products to all parts of the world.

We have very fond memories of our association as equal partners with Telemecanique for a long time. Two of their Senior Technical ManagerWs Mr. Flutch & Mr. Hammel and one from Marketing Mr. Hochet worked with us closely in the joint venture and I must say that there has been a lot we learned and gained mutually during this tenure. Even today we remain friendly forever.

Today we have designed and developed new series of Contactors ourselves and today we export our Contactors to more than 70 different countries. We are among the market leaders in India. Some of our products are also branded by other large Electrical Companies across the World. GE of USA uses our contactors in all the large Wind Mills they manufacture and install worldwide.

7. **SWITCHES. FUSES. SWITCH FUSE UNITS & CHANGEOVER SWITCHES 25A TO 3150A UNDER TECHNICAL COLLABORATION WITH STROMBERG OF FINLAND (1982-1987) :**

Sometimes opportunities do come knocking at your door and you do not realize and consider them as mere noise–to your disadvantage.

That is precisely what happened to us. In the late 1978 or so Mr. Passakivi from Finland visited us from the house of Wartsila trying to generate our interest in the Wartsila Range of Diesel Generating Sets imported from Finland.

Our hands were full of activity and we let this opportunity go over as Benares House who though not in the electrical field took over this project.

Mr. Passakivi who also spoke German Language besides English had become a very good friend. He visited and stayed in our home in Friends Colony at times and loved the Indian Culture. Surprisingly I noticed that some words in the Finnish Language come from the Hungarian Gypsies who originated from India.

Later in 1980 when we were interested in the very best Switch Fuse Units and Isolators our search focused finally on Stromberg–the Great Finnish Company.

I wrote to Mr. Passakivi who had retired by then. But his daughter having stayed in our house for a long time while she was studying the Indian History was very keen to invite our family to their house in Vasa for a Holiday.

In 1989 my wife Kanwal and I along with our children Radhika and Rishi landed at their house for the first time in Finland where we stayed for few days thoroughly enjoying their hospitality and culture.

We found the Finns as great people and we travelled with them far and wide in their beautiful country.

Finally on the pre-fixed meeting target date Mr. Passakivi himself drove me to the office of Stromberg – a most impressive and massive Plant at a grand location where they produced state of the art products with utmost proficiency. I returned to remember their magnitude and their proficiency in manufacturing.

They were new to India. Having Mr. Passakivi on our side was a very satisfying experience even for them since he had already visited our plants and could tell them about us in detail. Resultantly a Technical Collaboration Agreement was signed during that visit which got implemented thereafter.

With Terasaki Breakers already into our fold the Stromberg Range of Switch Fuse Units, Change-Over Switches and Isolators up to 3200 amps we were undoubtedly catering the best products in the Indian markets within this range.

I was keen to integrate these particular products which until then were the domain of the English Electric Company. We discovered Stromberg -Finland as being the world's largest and most competent manufacturers in this field. I travelled to Finland on a couple of occasions and the Finns were keen to join hands with us in the form of a technical collaboration for all other products as well. Later on however Stromberg was bought over by ABB–Switzerland & Sweden. Consequently we started manufacturing the Stromberg range of Switches, Fuses, Switch Fuse Units and Changeover Switches in India from 25A to 3150A.

Today we export these products around the world. We also design and manufacture some special Switches for ABB-Finland as well.

8. GENERATOR BUS DUCTS FOR GENERATORS UP TO 1000 MW UNDER TECHNICAL KNOWHOW FROM SIMELECTRO FRANCE (1983-1988) :

The desire to produce products where most other multinationals had not even reached used to engage my mind from the earlier days of our successful development of Naval Switchgear and Road Traffic Signals.

Discussing with my other friends from BHEL who were senior experts in High Voltage Switchgear I realized that Generator Bus Ducts i.e. large Bus Ducts that carry power from the terminals of a large Generator–say from 200 MW–1000 MW to the main Auxiliary Transformers, it was a very special aluminum welded and pressurized Duct of high value.

Until then these Ducts were the domain of companies like the BHEL and Best & Crompton in India till then. As more and more Power Plants came up, the demand had to be met from overseas. Leading players here were Simelectro of France, Alstom of France besides GE of USA, Hitachi of Japan and Siemens who were already on their own in India.

With a clear vision in my mind and on the basis of study of the market situation in India, I approached the House of Simelectro, France and convinced them to join hands with us for a technical collaboration.

A Group of engineers was selected especially for this purpose who were trained in France for six months in Design and Manufacturing Technologies. For the last 23 years now we are among the leaders today in the Indian market for the manufacture, supply, erection and commissioning of these Generator Bus Ducts not only for the prestigious Indian projects but we also export the same to neighbouring countries like Kuwait, Iran, Oman Bhutan etc. Simelectro meanwhile was bought over and have thence started operating in China.

Today we are rated as India's largest and most competent manufacturers of this product. Soon we hope to assume a similar position worldwide.

Having learnt the art of manufacturing High Voltage Bus Bars and after realizing that Low Voltage Bus Trunking systems were also the need of the hour for multistoried buildings as also for distribution of Power in large industrial houses, we engaged our engineers to design and develop special Low Voltage Bus Trunking systems both air-insulated and sandwiched parts of which we imported from Ciama, Spain. Ciama were later taken over by Siemens and resultantly we had to indigenize what all we were importing earlier from them.

Today we are the largest manufacturers of Low Tension Bus Bars in India and are the exclusive suppliers of the same to some of the most prestigious multistory buildings including the Indian Parliament House. We are also supplying them exclusively to large manufacturing units like Maruti, Hyundai, Honda etc. to name a few.

I make a mention to Michel Gaspard here – he was a great man and an equally great engineer who was the M.D of Simelectro France. He had meanwhile retired from his company. He was a great friend and he and his wife had even attended my children Radhika and Rishi's Weddings here in India. He was employed by us to evaluate Etacom of Belgium and later manage it for us as the CEO.

Years later in 2012 we also acquired the Etacom (of Belgium) who were the world leaders specialized in the Rasin Cast Bus Ducts for specialized requirements in Petro Chemical Industries.

Together with our Generator Bus Ducts, LV Bus Trunking and now the Resin Cast Bus Bars we have undoubtedly become the largest Bus Duct Manufacturers in the World with only the Chinese perhaps being similar in class and magnitude today.

9. FULL RANGE OF CONTROL & PROTECTION RELAYS IN JOINT VENTURE WITH SEG OF GERMANY (1991-2007) :

By the year 1992, I had realized that our Company had started manufacturing some of the most prestigious Components in the Low Voltage Switchgear field. The only product where we were depending upon English Electric Company (now known as Areva) was Power System Protection Relays. This was internationally the domain of Alstom-France or GEC of England and General Electric of USA, ABS of Germany & Sweden and Siemens-Germany etc. Most power projects in the country were delayed because of the large demand of these Relays and limited capacity of the manufacturers in India which were primarily the English Electric Company till then.

We connected with Mr. Schmidt, CMD of the house of SEG of Germany who had specialized in the latest Microprocessor controlled versions of such Relays. He hardly spoke any English, and my German language fluency came in very handy here! Soon we became close family friends visiting each other's factories etc.

Later we signed a joint venture with them to produce Micro Processor based Protection Relays in India in order to provide a more efficient and state-of-the-art technology in Power Protection and Control – as compared to the obsolete Electromagnetic Relays being used till then.

SEG were until then manufacturing Protection Relays which were mostly used in Diesel Generator Sets going up to a medium voltage–say up to 33 kV but not into large Power Plants of say 210 MW, 500 MW or 660 MW.

Our engineers worked in India along with the House of SEG-Germany and designed and manufactured special Relays which could then be used in large Power Projects putting us in direct competition with the likes of English Electric, Siemens, ABB, Alstom etc.

I am pleased to state that even this operation had been extremely successful.

Since SEG in Germany were later bought over by Cummins–another very large American Company, we had bought their shares in our Indian joint venture thereby completely bringing the Protection & Control Division to complement our C&S Products. Originally they had offered to buy us out – a proposition of which we did not accede since this complemented our product range. I then gave them a counter offer at the Hannover Fair and signed the deal there and then at the stalls of AVK SEG.

Today now this entire operation is being held and managed by our Company. Almost twelve leading design engineers under the stewardship of Prof. Srinivas and Prof. Karandikar, one of our senior design engineers, have further improved these Protection Relays which we also Brand and export out of India and use extensively in the Indian Power network today.

10. ALTERNATORS FROM 7.5 KVA- 5000 KVA IN JOINT VENTURE WITH AVK-GERMANY AND NOW WITH LEROY SOMER – FRANCE OWNED BY EMERSON NETWORK POWER PVT LTD, INDIA (2002-2009) :

Likewise in the year 1993 SEG-Germany with whom we had started manufacturing Electronic Protection Relays, were very impressed with our analytical design and manufacturing competence.

Mr Schnidt being a great friend of mine and ardent admirer of our Cooperation also offered to join hands with us to manufacture Alternators. It was a field in which they excelled right from 7.5 KVA to 20,000 KVA under the name AVK Avon Kaick.

I personally travelled to Germany with my team of engineers to AVK in order to study the intricate process of manufacturing these world class Brush Less Alternators and searched for the best technical expertise within India to manage such a specialized product range.

Finally we shortlisted and engaged Dr. S.K. Gupta, who used to head the Electrical Machines Business at BHEL Haridwar where they manufactured much larger Generators right up to 500 MW.

The Germans were indeed pleasantly surprised at the excellent technical team we had set-up. Our team was soon able to set-up a manufacturing project and start manufacturing Alternators to German designs with very little assistance from them except for a 3-weeks training which Dr. S.K. Gupta and his team had undergone in Germany during the initial period.

Even the first Alternator of 50 KVA built in our joint venture was 100% indigenous without any imported parts whatsoever. So successful has been this venture that we have been successfully exporting these Generators back to Germany.

In the year 2003 however AVK were bought over by Newage of U.K. belonging to the Cummins Group who likewise wanted to buy over the Company from us.

The Managing Director from Cummins was in a hurry to expand in India and made an offer to buy our shares. Having been successful in India and having generated core competence in numerous fields, we refused to sell our shares and instead bought them over to their complete surprise.

Later, Leroy Somer of France, the largest manufacturers of Generators in the world approached us and expressed their desire to become our partners. We appreciated this move and signed a joint venture agreement with them and the new company is now known as **Leroy Somer & Controls India (P) Ltd**. Some of our products have undergone changes to meet-up the demands of this new partner.

Today world-class Alternators are regularly being manufactured at our Works right from 2.5 KVA to 5000 KVA. We regularly export bigger machines from 500 KVA and above–to China, Singapore and South Africa etc.

Leroy Somer of France belong to the House of the 25 Billion Group called Emerson of USA. Besides owning Leroy Somer they also own two large Alternator manufacturing facilities in USA. So enamored have been Emerson and Leroy Somer with our technical competence, that a Design & Technical Centre has been opened at our Works with the primary task of working in line with USA and France to study the old designs of these machines and to make them more modern with greater efficiency and lesser costs.

Caterpillar of USA are exclusive customers of ours and all Caterpillar Machines made in India at their Hosur Plant near Bangalore are coupled with our Alternators. Besides, we are also the exclusive suppliers of Alternators to F.G. Wilson and Company in Coimbatore, who are the largest manufacturers of Generators in the world. Likewise, we supply Higher Capacity Alternators exclusively to Kirloskar Oil Engines Ltd. Pune.

11. COMPLETERANGEOFSCREWLESSCONNECTORS IN JOINT VENTURE WITH WAGO OF GERMANV SINCE 1995-2011 :

From the above story of the rise of our Company, it is evident that we realized during our earlier years that a 'Chain is only as strong as its weakest link'.

In the year 1966 when we started manufacturing Control Panels, we realized that good and properly made Terminal Blocks were not being manufactured in India and they were being imported from Germany. It was always on the back of my mind to sooner or later find a possibility of manufacturing world class Connectors in India.

In pursuit of this objective, in 1993, we signed a joint venture with world's largest producer of Screw Less Terminal Blocks named WAGO of Germany. WAGO are world leaders in the Fit and Forget variety where Terminals do not have to be tightened by screwing. Instead, a screw-driver is used to push the jaw which opens and locks the wire inside once the screwdriver is removed. These Terminal Blocks are extensively and exclusively being used today in the Indian Railways and also by the NTPC for their Power Plants and for Electronic and Electrical products throughout the country.

Our German partners are extremely happy with our competence and almost 100 verities of components are manufactured exclusively in India and re-exported to Germany from week to week.

12. A COMPREHENSIVE RANGE OF WORLD-CLASS LIGHTING ACCESSORIES, MODULAR SWITCHES, PLUGS & SOCKETS ETC. IN JOINT VENTURE WITH GEWISS-ITALY SINCE 2003-2008 :

Having succeeded and done very well in the field of Industrial Switchgear since 1966, in the year 2004 we approached the House of GEWISS-Italy who are the world leaders in the field of Modular Switches–the likes of which India had not seen till that date. These are the most exclusive and versatile range of domestic Switches, Plugs and Sockets as also Street Lighting Fittings, Flood Lights and some domestic lighting accessories manufactured by GEWISS in Italy.

I am pleased to state that these products are now being manufactured by us in India today for the last two years at our new plant at Haridwar in the State of Uttaranchal.

13. EXPORT ORIENTED UNIT (EOU) FOR GENERAL ELECTRIC OF USA SINCE 2003

Enamored by our manufacturing competence, the General Electric of U.S.A. selected our Company to manufacture some specific products for use by General Electric in U.S.A. especially for their Traction Equipment i.e. for use in Electric Locomotives exclusively manufactured by them for the entire U.S. market. Today, more than 100 specific products like Control Relays, D.C. Contactors and accessories etc. are being manufactured and shipped by us every month to the General Electric, U.S.A. which then get fitted into the most demanding Locomotives of the U.S. Railway System.

14. EXPORT ORIENTED UNIT (EOU) FOR EATON, U.K.

Our reputation in the field of manufacturing Electrical products has spread far and wide. Two years ago we were approached by the House of EATON of U.S.A. which is a USD 20 billion Group manufacturing Switchgear like we do. Their objective was two-fold -

(a) They wanted to outsource Motor Starters from India since they were not satisfied with the quality and cost of the products manufactured by themselves in U.K.

(b) They were not satisfied with the rising costs of MEM Switches & Sockets manufactured in the U.K. for over 8 decades.

We specially designed the Motor Starters according to the requisite dimensions which their engineers approved of, and today every month Motor Starters are being exported by us to the House of EATON in UK for the European market.

So satisfied were they with our quality and manufacturing capability that they asked their other Unit the famous MEM of UK which is one of their own manufacturing Company for domestic Switches, Plugs and Sockets to transfer their entire Plant and Machinery to us at NOIDA near Delhi. Today Switches, Plugs and Sockets worth more than RS. 2 crores per month are being sent back to them in the U.K.

More products from EATON are likely to join our manufacturing activities soon.

15. **DEVELOPMENT & MANUFACTURE OF SHOCK HARDENED SWITCHGEAR FOR THE INDIAN NAVY UNDER KNOWHOW FROM WHIPP & BOURNE, U.K. (1992-1997) :**

The Indian Navy short-listed our Company exclusively for developing and manufacturing Shock Hardened Switchgear for the first Indian Atomic Submarine. So satisfied was the Navy with what we had done for them over the last three decades, that they placed orders to indigenize and produce the first set of Switchgear and complete Switchboards and other Electricals for the first Indian Atomic Submarine–a project about which we were not supposed to be talking in earlier days but which is of common knowledge today.

Under know-how from the famous Whipp & Bourne of U.K, we designed and manufactured for the first time in India Shock

Hardened Air Circuit Breakers for AC and DC Applications operating up to 4000 which could withstand shock and vibration to the extent of 600g in the XYZ Axis.

It took us almost three years to design, manufacture and supply this entire range of equipment developed for the first time by any Indian Company in India. As a matter of fact, not more than 3-4 Companies around the world have been entrusted with such a task which has been accomplished by us most successfully.

16. LAST BUT NOT THE LEAST–A JOINT VENTURE WITH R.S. COMPONENTS, CORBY, U.K. (1994 - ONGOING SINCE OVER 25 YEARS NOW) :

In the year 1994, we signed a joint venture with R.S. Components in U.K. to supply world class Technical products in the category of Mechanical, Electric, Electronic and Pneumatic to the large spread of the Indian Industries across the Country through the mechanism of a large Catalogue of Products as was customary in Europe and America.

R.S. Components U.K. are the largest just-in-time suppliers of Components, stocking and selling more than 140,000 components to millions of customers throughout the world.

R.S. Components' Warehouses in U.K., Europe and in U.S.A. occupy 100,000 sq. ft. of covered area with large and modern stocking system which are fully computerized and picking and storing system which can boast of supply of parts and components to anywhere in the world within 24 hours.

Such a service was not known in India. Most Indian Industries, Utilities, Airports, Hospitals and Defence Institutions have suffered for years together and even had to write off equipment worth millions of Rupees because adequate imported spares within the time frame required were not available.

R.S. Components were most satisfied with our marketing and technical competence in this field.

In 1994 we formed a 50:50 joint venture which has developed

over the years the art of stocking and selling these products to more than 75,000 satisfied customers in India. Our sales offices today receive calls from our engineers spread throughout the length and breadth of India or even directly from customers.

Our offices are equipped to serve such vast clientele with a varied list of products within a period of 48 hours. We have a very large variety of satisfied customers right from the Defence Services to the Hospitality Industry, to the Airports and to each and every Industry worth its name in the Country.

17. J.V. WITH HIMOINSA of SPAIN (2006 – Ongoing Now with Yanmar of Japan)

The C&S Group has been pioneers in India in developing and introducing Sound Proof Diesel Generating Sets. It has revolutionized this industry which used to make leaky and noisy generating sets leading to wastage of energy and polluting the atmosphere throughout the country. Even the Government has come out with new Laws and Acts to prevent noise pollution and henceforth all Diesel Generators in India were to be manufactured with noise proof canopies to a sound level of maximum 72 decibel unlike the unwritten norms in the earlier days.

Capturing this opportunity and looking at the huge export market, we tied up with the world's 3rd largest manufacturer of Diesel Generating Sets namely HIMOINSA of Murcia, Spain.

A new Plant which is one of India's largest Generator Manufacturing Plant is currently being set up on a 48,000 sq yds of land at Rudrapur in Uttarkhand which will have a capacity of producing 5,000 assorted DG Sets in a year.

Today we are also exporting world class Sound Proof Gensets with Yanmar Engines to customers of Yanmar Overseas.

18. MEDIUM VOLTAGE SWITCHGEAR J.V. WITH EFACEC-PORTUGAL (2008 – 2013) :

Having so far mastered the manufacturing Technique to

produce highest quality of Low Voltage Switchgear equipment, I had realized that there is a scope in the Medium Voltage Sector where beyond the multinationals like Siemens, Schneider, ABB, Areva and BHEL, other Indian names are much smaller and insignificant.

We therefore in the year 2008 signed a joint venture with EFECEC of Spain–Portugal's largest Electrical Engineering Company manufacturing world class precision and quality Medium Voltage Switchgear up to 66 kV including Vacuum Breakers, SF6 Breakers, Switch Boards, Ring Main Units and High Voltage Transformers.

The new Manufacturing Plant is located in Greater Noida and is now being gradually shifted full scale to our 5 acre plot of land and an excellent building there upon to accommodate this project successfully.

In 2013 we had a friendly separation with EFACEC and we have now made substantial progress in marketing our own products in India and abroad.

19. FUTURE PROJECTS

Although most of our collaborations and joint ventures have already lapsed the agreed durations, C&S has always expressed its utmost appreciation and gratitude to all its former Technology Partners. We readily offer our Make in India world class Manufacturing Services and Products which are increasingly becoming more cost competitive and attractive worldwide today.

Having succeeded so far in our mission, our objective today is also to enter the area of Medium and High Voltage Switchgear so that we can be the first Indian Company to have a full range of Electrical products like the house of Siemens of Germany, GE of USA, ABB of Switzerland and other world leaders of this Industry. With such a strong foot hold in our manufacturing in India today, sky is indeed the limit by which we can grow and expand our markets worldwide ahead!

Chapter 6

The Purpose Of This Book Is Returning Back With Gratitude To The Society

The Purpose Of This Book Is Returning Back With Gratitude To The Society

The primary objective of writing and presenting this book is to serve the purpose of returning back with gratitude to the society from where I have gained substantially myself as an entrepreneur over my life span.

Returning back by a way of highlighting some of the commonly known age old virtues and Mantras of wisdom which I have personally relied upon, used and benefitted immensely from in my life – and which unfortunately and inadvertently do get diluted ignored and overlooked by most aspiring individuals as I observe today.

This book is therefore primarily intended to be my humble little contribution towards the success of all those daring optimists, self-starters, entrepreneurs and millions of all others who may likewise also choose for substantial and quantum gains & jumps in their lives or careers. They can benefit multifold in whatever activity position or profession they may be engaged in their lives today.

With such a staunch belief therefore, that a frank sharing of one's own experiences of successes and failures over a challenging life span is the best gift one can give back to the society, I am launching this book.

With such mutual integrity and expectations in our minds to gain and learn from this book therefore, my Dear Readers young, younger and the older, let us embark on this channel of communication and companionship between us.

This journey of rediscovering valued virtues stacked in our age old success Mantras in a relaxed style duly coupled with a live success story including corresponding interesting pictures thereof should undoubtedly and interestingly lead each and every one of you, my Dear Readers, to visualize and imagine seeing your own clearer lights at the end of your individual tunnels of effort and expectations in life.

In this unique manner you all also get to enjoy, imagine, visualize likewise and identify your own individual dreams and passions under your own specific conditions and circumstances no matter how big or small they may be.

This was the way I had tried myself and launched my mission one day as revealed in a brief step by step history of my professional development later in this book.

A journey perhaps through my own simple and interesting little life story duly assisted and guided by my Mantra collection may also excite and enable you to likewise imagine and motivate and ask your own self 'how soon one day you could also harness the tremendous potential that exists in each and every human being including you'.

My own first and initial Inspiration in my life for example comes from the undermentioned simple Mantra I learned and their significance I grasped from my revered father The Late Mr. Justice P.N. Khanna at my early age of 7 to 8 years only when I was in my School Class 3.

"Heights *by Great Men Reached and Kept;*

Were never attained by sudden Flights

But they while their companions slept

Were toiling upwards in the Nights"

My Dear Readers I have therefore specially compiled for you A TREASURE BOX of Mantras I collected over my life.

Soon you will also enjoy and realize that such a TOOL-KIT when used by you yourself, will also enthuse and lead you interestingly towards achieving your own goals. You will lead a better satisfied and more successful life ahead.

As you move from one Mantra to the other their words shall be like compassionate reminders to reaffirm the frozen value and wisdom contained therein to make you enjoy, feel, believe and say to yourself -

I can do it too!!

Chapter 7

Don't We All
Deserve To Feel Happy &
Accomplished In Our Lives
Rediscover And Rekindle
Your Own Natural Power To
Uplift Yourself Stop Loosing
The Fire In Your Belly
For Achieving A Great &
Successful Life You All
Deserve.

Don't We All Deserve To Feel Happy & Accomplished In Our Lives Rediscover And Rekindle Your Own Natural Power To Uplift Yourself Stop Loosing The Fire In Your Belly For Achieving A Great & Successful Life You All Deserve.

Yes indeed this book My Friends is all about getting clear and clearer in your minds that -

We All Deserve to Feel Happy.

We All Deserve to Start Feeling, Witnessing and Enjoying Happiness in Our Lives.

We All Therefore Do Wish to Know the Simplest Route to Develop the Know-how to Create Happiness & Contentment in Our Lives Ahead.

Therefore let us first accept and realize that we all i.e. each and every one of us are in fact born as genius by nature. We are possessing the God given gift of a natural power to uplift our lives to achieve the target or the goal we may choose to set for ourselves for our ultimate happiness.

Sadly however most of us do not recognize and utilize this God given gift of the power to excel in our lives. We merely surrender ourselves or choose to live and finish as mediocre or poor and unhappy only.

Therefore, STOP becoming a victim of fate ONLY which many of us unfortunately DO.

STOP therefore, even meekly surrendering your lives to mere mediocrity.

STOP Loosing the fire in your bellies which is there for achieving a great and successful life ahead.

Develop instead the hunger in your bellies – hunger for

achieving genuine excellence, pleasure and satisfaction in whatever big or small you undertake.

Develop confidence and do not ever be shy to be your own original self.

It is not difficult at all to develop this self-confidence as you will read and feel for yourself in the pages following.

Do not let your past failures lead you to surrender yourself desperately to fate.

Do not ever surrender yourself dejectedly by choosing a living merely for the sake of it.

Let your past failures teach and motivate you to build yet a new dream and a fresh desire to uplift your life ahead for your own good.

Have a little patience and start believing in yourself. Your betterment will come soon by the simple step by step route shown in this book.

This book will highlight in a simple step by step manner the importance of thinking, planning, directing and committing yourself to a path you may choose to adopt in life for your ultimate success.

With such a positive belief in yourself, simply enjoy reading this book to reach your goal – feeling happy and victorious which you obviously deserve to be.

Now hold your breath and jump in for a highly motivating and enjoyable experience for quantum betterment in your life ahead.

Chapter 8

Whatever Be Your Current Situation This Book can Now Become Your Ready Reckoner Your Simple Success Mantra Tool Kit (SSMTK) for Your Ultimate Success.

Whatever Be Your Current Situation This Book can Now Become Your Ready Reckoner Your Simple Success Mantra Tool Kit (SSMTK) for Your Ultimate Success.

No matter whether you are an ordinary young or grown up student, a worker, an employee, a teacher, a shopkeeper, a farmer or a small scale employer, a big businessman, or whatever and wherever you may be.

No matter what be your current position, situation, condition or circumstances.

No matter how small or big an occupation you may be handling today–in any and every profession and walk of life.

It is totally wrong to believe that the good, big, and great things can only happen when you have a big office, a big bank balance, or a big title.

No, No, No, Please!

All This Is Not Necessary

Your need is to -

START Today – Not TOMORROW

No More Waiting For Some Imaginary

Brighter Time Later In Future.

So always utilize your current position and your current platform to rise up and above in life.

We all must clearly understand, strongly believe and realize for our own good – the simple age old saying,

'A Bird In Hand Is Always Better Than Two In The Bush'.

Therefore our current position in life – no matter how

small, trivial, insignificant or big whatever it may be – is the bird in our hands.

Let this be your first, best and ready platform to rise in your life.

Let this be your perfect platform for building your own self confidence day by day in order to improve your own life further.

Therefore, start today!

Whatever and wherever you are is definitely good enough to start and improve your life step by step further.

Utilizing your own inherent internal potential that we all possess without exception including you.

Your own internal potential is longing to come out to help you.

Your own potential is powerful.

You may really, unfortunately and unknowingly be overlooking it currently without recognizing and appreciating its true worth.

Let this book become your own success Mantra TOOL-KIT, your own ready reckoner for your own definite success hence forward.

All this and much more you will soon enjoy discovering, after reading a few pages of this book.

Believe in yourself and very soon you will develop the confidence which you will interestingly start feeling and using.

Chapter 9

Who Is Responsible For Your Life Today?

Who Is Responsible For The Position You Command In Your Life Today?

Who Is Responsible For Your Life Today? Who Is Responsible For The Position You Command In Your Life Today?

Your Destiny

Your Genes, Your Faith,

Your Father, Your Mother,

Your Wife, Your Husband,

Your Teacher, Your Boss,

Your Country, Your Government

Or Your Same Old Blame Game?

They did not do this for me, they hurt and insulted me...

Each time you say these lines, you merely fool your own self to falsely believe in them.

As if others created Your Destiny;

As if others created Your Failures;

As if others created Your Success?

The fact however is that,

You alone are the creator of your own Destiny, your Life your Successes, your Failures and your Life Ahead.

Take Things In Your Own Hands

Take Responsibility

And Everything Will Fall In Line.

Chapter 10

What is a Mantra?

How Best to Recite & Use the Mantras

What Is A Mantra?

How Best To Recite & Use The Mantras.

Mantra is a sacred old Sanskrit word used in our Shastras (sacred texts) and Vedas since thousands of years in India for self-inspiration.

The Word Mantra is Composed of Two Parts:

Mana – Meaning The Mind and

Tra – Meaning A Vehicle, Tool or an Instrument To Tune & Transport Our Mind's Message To Action & Accomplishment.

Mantra

Mantras have also been used for Transcendental Meditation & Motivation for Centuries.

Mantras are time tested simple words of prudence.

They are the quotes for success and provide almost magical motivation to overcome your hurdles in life towards achieving your ultimate happiness and accomplishment of Goals of your lives.

Mantras enthuse you and brighten your moment to navigate and elevate you through the ups & downs of life.

Mantra is a rhythmic short statement that uses positive and uplifting words to create a positive, constructive and an uplifting mindset.

Mantra can be a phrase or even a sentence using vital chosen words of wisdom which you can conveniently recite to yourself with a rhyme or otherwise as you deem fit to, convey a message to your conscience.

Mantras enhance and improve your own well-being whenever

you need an instant PICK-UP.

How to Use & Recite Your Mantra

In order for the Mantras to be increasingly effective, they need to be read and said slowly with a relaxed but strong powerful feeling, and a strong belief behind them.

Recite your Mantras slowly and try to put in a lot of belief and feeling into the words that you say for a strong positive effect on your conscience and to accomplish your own chosen wish in life.

Try to choose the Mantra you feel is most suited to your own circumstances and try to recite it daily – morning and evening as many times as your time permits for that optimum effect.

All the Mantras compiled by me in this book have been derived by me from my Mentors as also through my own experiences of a life time.

You may also flexibly amend and alter them to suit your own rhythm and your own personal and specific needs or conditions to meet your aspirations.

Mantras can be used as instruments to free your mind from stress, from doubts and fears duly replacing them with hope positivity and action driven thoughts.

By investing a few minutes only on your own chosen Mantras, every morning and night or even at lunch break and working hours, you will be amazed to feel and experience enormous uplifting benefits in your life.

With every breath you inhale and exhale while completing and reciting your Mantra you will increasingly feel more relaxed and confident.

You may also visualize and feel the gradual melting away of your tensions bringing in a wave of enthusiasm in your conscience.

Recite the Mantra slowly and at an enjoyable pace say 5 Times every day either loudly or quietly to yourself as you get up in the morning and before you go to bed at night.

You may even find it beneficial for you to keep a written copy of your chosen Mantra for spontaneous reach.

It can be in a written and folded leaf in your wallet, your laptop, your desk top, your mobile phone, your car, your bed room or bathroom or wherever you find it convenient.

This will be your best ready reckoner allowing you to effectively work its handy magic to you.

The vibrations that a Mantra creates can change how you activate your reality shift, your mindset and create a new positive belief about your own self.

Repeating a chosen Mantra regularly can help your brain rewire your mindset.

Learning is known as the daughter of repetition. Keep repeating in your own mind what you have decided to learn and practice in your life.

Repetition is the powerful tool technique and tactic of all successful people.

Through repetition new ideas get integrated into beliefs.

Our own motivating and highly successful Mantra -

We can do it – We shall do it – We will do it

We repeat this on our each Annual Meeting and also in between for its own tried worth.

Beliefs can charge up the way to action and direction to achieving your goals.

Summing up the success Mantra's positive effect

Success Mantras can work wonders to boost your concentration and focus.

Success Mantras can lower your heart rate and blood pressure ultimately balancing your body.

Success Mantras can help you relieve the feeling of stress or frustration.

Success Mantras can teach you to find love and compassion for yourself and others.

Success Mantras give you the strength, the inspiration and the enthusiasm to lead a positive purposeful and joyous life, no matter what be your current position or circumstances.

Success Mantras can stimulate the energy chakras in your mouth and throat enabling you to express yourself better.

Therefore why not give your chosen success Mantra a chance?

Enjoy witness & watch how wonderfully this experience changes your life journey – meaningfully, accomplishedly and happily for all times ahead.

Chapter 11

How Visualization Of Any Success Story Covered With A Spread Of Related Photographs And Reciting Of Selected Motivating Mantras Can Be An Inspiring, Enjoyable And Relaxed New Route To Trigger Your Own Internal Urge To Achieve And Your Own Potential For Your Growth And Success

How Visualization Of Any Success Story Covered With A Spread Of Related Photographs And Reciting Of Selected Motivating Mantras Can Be An Inspiring, Enjoyable And Relaxed New Route To Trigger Your Own Internal Urge To Achieve And Your Own Potential For Your Growth And Success

Unlike mundane prose and epic antics sometimes preached and used in such books, my attempt in this book on the contrary is to relate a simple ideology in a simple language, revealing clearly a true account which you must read and feel to believe.

My attempt in this book is to share my life-long thoughts & experiences with you in a totally unique productive and relaxed new style.

I have therefore purposely included some related old photographs covering my life span from eight to eighty years.

Likewise I have included some of the motivating success Mantras I myself have used benefitted and relied upon in my life.

By visualization I simply mean to convey that each one of you My Dear Readers, should imagine in your minds how it will feel when you succeed in achieving your dream or goal in life.

Do not at all hesitate – Do not feel shy – Just do it.

Your own efforts when combined with visualization will accelerate manifolds to make your dream come true.

With every breath you inhale and exhale while completing and reciting your Mantra, you will feel increasingly more relaxed and confident.

You may also visualize and feel the gradual melting away of your tensions bringing in a wave of enthusiasm in your conscience.

Recite the Mantra slowly and at an enjoyable pace say 5 times either loudly or quietly to yourself as you get up in the morning or before you go to bed in the night.

You may even find it beneficial for you to keep a written copy of your chosen Mantra for spontaneous reach out. A written and folded leaf inside your wallet, your laptop, desk top, mobile phone, your car, your bed side table or bathroom or at any other place you find convenient.

This will be your best ready reckoner allowing you to really work its handy magic on you.

The vibrations that a Mantra creates can change how you activate your reality shift, your mindset and emerge winner with a new positive belief about your own self.

Repeating a chosen Mantra regularly can help your brain rewire your mindset.

Remember that learning is always the daughter of repetition. Keep repeating in your own mind what you have decided to learn and practice in your life.

Repetition is a powerful tool, technique and tactic of all successful people.

Through repetition new ideas get integrated into beliefs.

My Suggestion is that you please simply try to create a picture in your mind of what you really wish and want in Life. Simultaneously also please also try generating even if an imaginary feeling of your having achieved the desired wish as well.

Olympic Athletes are trained to run or swim with the imagination of the true events in their minds. They are taught that if you can develop a feeling of a real good performance or a win in your mind while training, you are very likely to do it likewise also in the real event as well.

Same is the reality in life where we notice around us that most results and outcomes having been created or invented are so because one person amongst us was able to see a clear picture in his mind of the end result he wanted.

The rest is his hard work, team work and other actions, combined with the forces of Universe which augmented his efforts to fetch the end results into his lap.

With such a picture in your mind when you start visualizing towards the end result of your dream, you will also achieve it more easily combined with your own efforts than without it.

Besides visualization of your wishes or accomplishments you must also develop a feeling of abundance and joyfulness being created with your accomplishment. This is another important positive feeling and thought which also contributes towards accelerating your fulfillment.

As a matter of fact whether we admit or not each and every one of us do visualize. However, because of a self-ordained feeling of shyness in our own minds we do not admit it.

Such shyness needs to be boldly replaced with fondness and expectance and you will realize wonders will happen to accelerate the accomplishment of your dreams.

The power of visualization for success and gathering enthusiasm and affirmations for success through Meditation and Mantras with their frozen wisdom embedded therein has always led to self-motivation and accomplishment of one's desires, cravings and dreams.

However ownership of such a realization has so far been missing and not so openly understood, accepted and preached.

Visualization of your dreams transfers into thoughts. Thoughts lead to action and action leads us to corrections in course if necessary for achieving ultimate success in our lives.

This book may enable you to visualize some of my own experiences in a live interesting and relaxed manner. Interestedly viewing the enclosed photographs may also lead you to draw your own inferences and conclusions in the situations you foresee and seek for yourself under your own respective circumstances.

You may also find it very interesting to select and identify a Mantra which somewhat rhymes and answers your own challenges. Feel free, and enjoy reading aloud even, chanting the same with or without your own alterations to enthuse & motivate yourself at any particular stage in your life.

Gradually such a Mantra will enter your sub-consciousness and you will keep repeating reciting & enjoying it with simultaneous requisite visualization, motivation and action towards achieving your own Goals or successes you all deserve.

Chapter 12

How My Simple Success Mantra Tool Kit (SSMTK) The Operating System For Referable Wisdom Can Lead You To Build More Meaningful Successful And Happier Lives Ahead

How My Simple Success Mantra Tool Kit (SSMTKT) The Operating System For Referable Wisdom Can Lead You To Build More Meaningful Successful And Happier Lives Ahead

From my early childhood to the present day in my own amateurish way I have been noting collecting and scribbling in my old diaries and note books some Quotes & Mantras that impressed me and have left an indelible mark on my psyche.

This has evolved in generating my own operating system of precious referable Quotes, Mantras and Words of Wisdom which I have always employed and experimented within my life.

In doing so naturally I have drawn upon the wealth of some old Quotes and Mantras that have enthused and encouraged me in my business & personal life over the years.

Mantras & Metaphors that I learnt from my Revered father Late Mr. Justice Prem Nath Khanna, my professors at the IIT Kharagpur, and from my colleagues & professors in Germany where I worked and learned during my formative years.

My collections are also from numerous Indian & Overseas Business Leaders and Collaborators with whom I've had the fortune of dealing with over the last 50 years. In addition also are those gathered from several illustrious books I have read and consulted from time to time within my life span.

A journey through my own reasonably challenging, interesting, successful and rewarding life span duly coupled with a few chronologically placed photographs plus reading through my success Mantra Tool-kit should also excite and enable you to likewise visualize, motivate and ask your own self 'how soon one day you can also harness the tremendous potential that always exists in each and every human being including you'.

You will be surprised to know that my own first and initial inspiration in my own life, for example, came from the undermentioned simple but one of the most powerful success oriented Mantra which I learned and understood from my revered father,

"Heights by Great Men Reached and Kept;
Were never attained by sudden Flights
But they while their companions slept
Were toiling upwards in the Nights"

Every evening when our father returned home from his office, among other stories and news of the day were exchanged. This was also the most exciting time when we repeated this success Mantra. I learnt this Mantra by heart and I would keep on reciting it to my own self in my own little privacy everywhere. No wonder it naturally left a lasting impression on my life throughout.

My Dear Readers I have therefore specially compiled for you A TREASURE BOX of success inducing, highly interesting and motivating Mantras collected over my life span.

Many of these acquired self-inducing and motivating Mantras I have quietly and personally been using from my early childhood days to invigorate my own confidence and conscience. I must confess that all these have undoubtedly and greatly helped me at different stages in my own life for developing and purposely shaping up my own career.

Today therefore, I wish to boldly recommend this well-practiced success Mantra Tool-Kit to you all with an absolutely clear intent to help and assist you in your lives ahead.

These success Mantras should undoubtedly give you a fighting chance to raise your own enthusiasm and that of your team with whom you work and even that of your family members including children and grand-children. Also in general with Institutions, Societies & localities you may be exposed to–wherever you wish to improve their lots.

Some over proud and conceited people may even discard these age old metaphors and words of wisdom as only a bunch of crap.

All I can say for such people is that in trying to satisfy and boost their lowly pride and ego they sometimes don't even know what they are missing out on. God Bless Them!

Many of my own friends, my children and grand-children and other family members, my Business Associates and colleagues at various levels and our staff have realized the worth of these Words of Wisdom. The success Mantra Tool-Kit has already been shared with them through Leaflets, formally and informally or verbally from time to time.

Soon you will also enjoy and realize that such a success Mantra TOOL-KIT when used by you yourself, will also lead you most interestingly towards achieving more satisfied and successful lives ahead.

As you move from one success Mantra to another their words shall be like compassionate reminders to reaffirm the frozen value and wisdom contained therein to make you enjoy, feel, believe and succeed.

Success Mantras and old and new quotations always give you a great sense of assurance and hope that there is merit and value in their well proven messages.

Even when you are in a fix and fail to understand a given situation in your life, a most relevant Mantra can come to your rescue and enthuse you to say:

"My Goodness

I Can Do it Too!"

You may also find it very interesting and motivating to read each Mantra and enjoy identifying the one that somewhat answers your own challenges in life at a particular stage – even by reading it a little loud in your own privacy or together with your team.

Life may at times be Not All That Smooth.

Even the wisest of us can find it Difficult To Handle.

There are hurdles in the journey of life sometimes but There Is Always A Way Out.

However those who take time and those who care to understand the value of these Mantras of easy understandable wisdom will always see the light at the end of the tunnel, find their way out of any dark tunnel – to their absolute freedom, success, safety and happiness all the way ahead.

Therefore to sum up this vital chapter here is a valuable old Mantra full of truth & wisdom most appropriate for this occasion.

"Men Consume Their Lives in Vague Pursuits
But Those Whom Truth & Wisdom Lead
Can Gather Honey from the Weed".

My Dear Readers - This Is The Essence And The Fact of Life.

My Simple Success Mantra Tool Kit

(SSMTK)

Mantra 1

God Helps Those Who Help Themselves

God Helps Those Who Help Themselves.

(Narrated and explained to me by my revered Father when I was only 8 Years Old in 1948 in Mussoorie.)

God helps those who help themselves.

This is undoubtedly one of the most precious and meaningful old Mantras-generally well known to most people around the world.

Yet most people tend to overlook and therefore even fail to appreciate the true message, the meaning, the depth, the worth and the wisdom contained and embedded into this great Mantra.

We must recognize how clearly this great Mantra highlights the significance of our own efforts, and our self-help which essentially needs to be coupled with our prayers to create the end result we are looking for and not merely our prayers without our inputs.

Our prayers are thus offered to our Lord God seeking his blessings for the wisdom, the strength and the power to pursue and achieve desired success in our objectives with our own inputs, our own determined efforts and hard work and not without it.

Our prayers therefore must not be mistaken as a mere surrender to fate and destiny expecting our Lord God instead to undertake all the hard work meant for us – the Recipients without our Karma and Action.

Banda Na Kare Bhajan

To Bhagwan Kya Kare

This has been very aptly explained by our Revered Gurujee,

The Learned Shree Venugopal Goswamiji.

Bhajan signifies our action and Karma commensurate with the success we seek.

"Nothing Comes From Nothing

Nothing Ever Could"

One can't go back and change the beginning of one's life and one's Karma or actions in the past already over and gone by - but one can most certainly and always start afresh in the present wherever you are and in whichever situation you are, and start for changing your future ending in the days ahead with your fresh and determined Karmas and actions.

This should be our motto and purpose in life which will boost our inherent internal potential manifolds.

The Great God Of Multitude Teachings, Messages And Blessings Embedded In Lord Ganesha's Auspicious Appearance Itself.

The Big Forehead	Signifies	Develop Your Intellect
Big Ears & Small Mouth	"	Hear More & Speak Less
The Big Trunk	"	Wisdom To Discriminate Between Right & Wrong
One Leg & Foot Pointing Upwards	"	Towards The Heaven We All Wish To Acuire
The Second Leg & Foot On Ground	"	Thinking Of Heaven Yet Being Firmly On Ground.
Big Belly	"	Digesting All Kinds Of Experiences, Ego & Difficulties
Abundance Of Food In Front Of Lord Ganesha	"	Material Wealth, Power & Prosperity
The Tiny Rat Looking At The Lord, Not The Food	"	Greed In All Human Beings But It Is To Be Kept Under Control

The Lord's Four Arms signify The Four Inner Possessions – the subtle Body comprising - Mind, Intellect, Ego and Consciousness. Ganesha himself represents the Atman, the soul which enables these four possessions to function properly

Mantra 2

Lord Ganesha The Ultimate Lord & Mantra Of Multitude Teachings & Blessings When Understood And Practiced Brings Ultimate Success & Peace In Life

Lord Ganesha The Ultimate Lord & Mantra Of Multitude Teachings & Blessings When Understood And Practiced Brings Ultimate Success & Peace In Life.

All over India most of us worship Lord Ganesha throughout our lives as the most auspicious and beloved Deity, bringer of peace and prosperity. All our prayers on all occasions start with the worship of Lord Ganesha. Beautiful statues and carvings of Lord Ganesha decorate the entrance of many houses, offices and factories as well.

Yet most of us forget the precious message and teachings enshrined and embedded in Lord Ganesha's appearance itself which is therefore briefly highlighted hereunder for your reckoning and awakening again.

Ganesha is a Sanskrit word.

Gana in Sanskrit means 'multitude' and 'esha' means 'The Lord'. Ganesha therefore means the Lord God of multitude blessings and teachings, 'the Lord of all beings'.

Ganesha is the son of Lord Shiva who in fact represents the supreme reality.

Why is Ganesha elephant faced, what all he is holding in his hands and why is the little mouse sitting underneath–are all symbolic representations of Vedic teachings to ordinary human beings which if followed, can lead to ultimate happiness.

The Ethos Of The Hindu Religion And Body Mind Intellect Syndrome

The ultimate happiness as per the age old ethos of the Indian Vedic philosophy, comes from the realm and belief that human life is composed of three important elements – the body, the mind & the intellect.

When we are born, God gives us the body and the body has a mind. The mind is generally wavering in different directions and cannot deliver the ultimate happiness unless we develop the intellect to control the mind.

There are certain simple methods of developing intellect and happiness. These methods have been frozen in the shape of Lord Ganesha.

Why the elephant? Because the elephant has a big forehead, teaching us to develop intellect to control our mind.

Elephant has big ears and a small mouth – telling us to hear more and speak less.

The trunk which springs from Ganesha's head represents the intellect, the faculty of discrimination which necessarily arises out of wisdom. Thus the trunk has the wisdom and the discrimination to choose to lift a small pin or uproot a complete tree.

Lord Ganesha sits with one leg folded and other down, pointing towards the heaven and earth – meaning thereby that think of heaven but do not forget that you are still on the earth.

Lord Ganesha has a large belly conveying that a man of perfection can consume and digest whatever experiences he undergoes. Heat or cold, war or peace, birth or death and other such trials and tribulations do not toss him up and down. Figuratively, he is represented as being able to stomach and digest all types of experiences – pleasant and unpleasant.

The tiny rat looking up towards Lord Ganesha is the symbol of greed in man. There is a lot of food lying around at the feet of the Lord and yet the rat is not eating anything but sitting under full control watching the Lord. Every human being has greed but the greed must be under control.

Lord Ganesha has four arms. The four arms represent the four inner properties and powers of the subtle human body. These are, Mind, Intellect, Pride and Consciousness. Lord Ganesha represents all these in pure consciousness – as we call it the Atman or the Soul which empowers and enables these four powers to function in YOU.

The details of Lord Ganesha's description suggest deep philosophical significance which can guide us all to reach a supreme state of human perfection.

No wonder over the years, Lord Ganesha has become symbolic of happiness, success and prosperity.

These are some of the teachings which ordinary men forget. Therefore our forefathers, the clever older generation were wise enough to freeze them in the form of a figure so that if we keep such a figure anywhere in the house, office or for that matter at any place it will remind us of the teachings which when followed and practiced by us will bring the ultimate happiness.

Mantra 3

Heights By Great Men Reached & Kept Were Never Attained By Sudden Flights – But While Their Companions Slept They Were Toiling Upwards In The Nights

Heights By Great Men Reached & Kept Were Never Attained By Sudden Flights – But While Their Companions Slept They Were Toiling Upwards In The Nights.

(Dale Carnegie Through my Revered Father in 1948 when I was 8)

Like the first two great Mantras, you may have read already that the Mantra No. 3 here as above was the next most important learning from my Revered Father.

The true significance of this Mantra "Toiling upwards in the nights" is that in the peace and calm of nights or early morning when most others are sleeping, the ones who wish to attain great heights in life must think, dream, plan and act for their lives ahead not leaving it merely to the mercy of the Lord to decide for them.

Without well thought of ideas and a concrete aim or life plan you are like a ship drifting aimlessly in the sea. You will only go where the tide takes you. You are like a leaf floating in the air not knowing where to settle.

Such a life cannot provide happiness and fulfillment for which we all live and yearn for.

Therefore, we need to take up and develop our own original ideas which means marking and even writing them down as a kind of mission statement defining the purpose and objective of the life you wish to lead.

Something that inspires you to your dreams, ideas and desires which you keep further clarifying, shaping, firming and re-writing as you grow in your life with more and more exposure and time.

Such an idea or a mission statement essentially helps you to keep concentrating in your mind and taking small steps and actions that are most important to achieve your mission, your goal in life. Such a mission statement also awakens your own sub-conscious mind which by the law of Nature also helps you immensely to achieve your dream with your efforts.

This actually happens every day in life and this is not fiction.

The journey of a life span begins always with such a simple single step. You must start off small if you wish to build on big results tomorrow.

Such a mission statement becomes your own powerful compass to keep your life pointed towards your goal in life all the time.

If I look at my own case after our family had lost almost all our material possessions and family wealth during the partition of India in 1947, living in the small rented house in Mussoorie Hills the above Mantras indeed gave me a purpose in life, even at a rather early age.

With such a deep thinking to regain our lost position I decided to do away with my century old family's legacy of law & judiciary and instead made my mission to become an engineer and an industrialist one day.

The journey of a thousand miles always begins with a small step if you want big results to follow.

What you focus on earlier in life always shapes your future.

Take Up An Idea

Think Of It

Dream Of It

Make It Your Goal In Life

Go To Bed Thinking Of It

Get Up from bed thinking of It

Keep Working on it Relentlessly

You Will Undoubtedly Achieve

It Sooner Than Later.

(Swami Vivekanand through My Revered Father in 1949 when I was 9)

My revered father explained the common objective of the above two Mantras was almost identical.

With whatever little understanding one had at that young age, the repeated recitement of these two Mantras had a very meaningful initial inspiration in my mind which got further clarified and I understood the worth of these words.

I for instance had then made up my mind to become an industrialist one day. The rest of my life has been derived from this objective gained at an early age.

Mantra 4

ENTHUSIASM IS LIKE FILLING GOD IN YOU -

LIFE WITHOUT ENTHUSIASM IS LIKE SODA WITHOUT FIZZ

ENTHUSIASM Is Like Filling God In You
Life Without Enthusiasm Is Dull As Soda Without Fizz.

Dale Carnegie used to say -

"If you cannot give your child a gift then give her or him one thing and everything else will follow automatically and that one thing is Enthusiasm".

Enthusiasm comes from the Latin Word 'En (to fill in)' and 'Theo (God)'.

Enthusiasm–is therefore like filling God in you.

With God in you and your dedicated efforts, you will always succeed.

Life without Enthusiasm is dull & monotonous. Just like soda without fizz & bubbles is boring and isn't acceptable.

Similarly life without enthusiasm & zest is boring and incomplete.

Therefore, think enthusiastically – if you want to succeed. Enthusiasm rids your mind of worries and tensions.

Enthusiasm ventilates your mind and makes it more positive and productive.

The stronger is your desire and your enthusiasm to achieve, the stronger is the signal to your sub-conscience to act and achieve and resultantly you do achieve.

Let your Enthusiasm always be infectious and even contagious.

Infect all those you meet with appreciation and enthusiasm. Enthuse your followers, fellow colleagues, team mates, your family members and your friends.

Get enthused and excited in life about success, about happiness, about all your personal goals and you will achieve all of them.

Take up all your work yourself with your team with excitement and joy and you will soon see success will come naturally with joy and satisfaction to all.

When your enthusiasm starts to blossom, your passion and empathy about your job and tasks that are there in front of you also blossoms.

No longer will you feel like a leaf floating in the wind with no control over your time and your life. Instead you will be committed to direction of your choice.

No longer will you feel that you never had enough time to do things you loved to do.

You also need to nurture and fill your well of enthusiasm and inspiration every day. Because challenges of life may to some extent drain that inspiration which needs rebuilding each day.

There was a man who made a living selling balloons at a fair. He had all nice colours, like the blue, green, red and yellow.

Occasionally the Balloon Man would release one helium filled balloon up in the air to attract more and more children.

One day he felt his jacket tugged at. It was a little boy who held one white balloon in his one hand. He was looking at the man's balloons with fascinated eyes, 'I have a white balloon. But it doesn't go that high. Which is the best colour that will fly higher?' he asked.

Moved by the boy's innocence the man replied, 'Son it is not the colour of the balloon. It is what's filled inside that makes it go up'.

The same thing applies to your life. And that one thing is your enthusiasm within you that will make you rise.

Once that inside is triggered with your enthusiasm you will realize how very far you can sail in life.

Abraham Lincoln who was clearly one of the greatest among American Presidents said,

'Without Him I cannot succeed
& With Him I cannot fail.'

He used to say that the same holds good and true with enthusiasm also –

'Without Enthusiasm I cannot succeed
& With Enthusiasm I cannot fail.'

We all can adopt this wonderful thought blending the two ideologies.

Try it and feel the difference.

We all can do it – try it and feel the difference.

Mantra 5

Dream – Desire– Direction & Commitment Using The D3 & C Formula The Well Tried & Proven Formula For Guaranteed Success In Your Lives Your success is written on the wall, go and grab

Dream – Desire–Direction & Commitment Using The D3 & C Formula The Well Tried & Proven Formula For Guaranteed Success In Your Lives. Your success is written on the wall, go and grab.

(Through Professor Muller Wuppertal Germany 1962)

Dreaming

Dreaming is one of the most essential and important part of our lives and must not be simply discarded and stopped merely because some wrongly understood old dogmas suggest to stop dreaming and start working instead. This amounts to putting the cart before the horse.

It is the birth right of every human being to have dreams. Life without dreams will be dull & boring.

So build-up a strong and well considered dream. Soon you will realize that this dream will build you.

Dream freely and intently of your own successful self as you wish to become one day.

Desire

By this process of sincere dreaming you will undoubtedly and naturally develop a very deep & keen internal desire to achieve your dream one day.

Direction

By the Universal Law of Nature this deep and sincere desire will always lead you to finding the directions or the route to your dreamt and desired success.

Commitment

Now go on and adopt this direction–understand the logic and commit yourself to follow the path this direction indicates. Soon you will yourself notice the small successes of your efforts shall start showing up. These successful outcomes will step by step accelerate gradually to enable you achieve your ultimate bigger dream.

Dreaming of success and acquiring success is a journey and not a destination and you will keep dreaming bigger and achieving higher with the passage of time.

For this to happen all you need to do is take time to introspect – go within yourself to set up something like a goal or a target for the kind of success that you dream of achieving in your life at present.

Make this simple and easy experiment in your lives. Realize that it is important not to merely live for the sake of it but instead for living your own dreamt of, superior and a substantially better and fulfilling life ahead.

The journey you will notice is easy and highly self-motivating and enjoyable.

Develop your own self-confidence gradually and continue on this journey of success, dream and desire in small steps. It can then be accelerated to achieve your ultimate bigger goal and much more in your life ahead.

It is not that things and opportunities we wish and want do not exist. They always do.

Once that inside in you is triggered with your commitment, fresh enthusiasm will be generated and you will realize how very far you can sail in life.

Therefore & until we read such books we are not even aware that all possibilities and wishes we have, can and will get manifested for each and every one of us in our lives.

Besides generating your own internal inspirations through your own processing of your Dreams Desires Direction and commitment explained above, you may also find a lot of inspiration from others to build your own dreams.

Whereas my Dear Readers the inspiration can come from external sources.

Life ends when you Stop Dreaming

Hope ends when you Stop Believing

Love ends when you Stop Caring

So Dream Hope and Love

With The Right Karma and Action

To Make Your Life Beautiful.

I did realize while hearing and learning from Dr. Mueller that the formula 3D&C was only a refined and a very much clear version of the Mantras 3 & 4 leading to the requisite desired direction only. This indeed further reaffirmed my own conviction to start one day on my own and proceed not knowing however when, where and how.

Mantra 6

How True Magic & Success Will Unfold In Your Lives Once You Accept Responsibility You Alone Are Responsible For The Way Your Life Is Placed Currently

How True Magic & Success Will Unfold In Your Lives Once You Accept Responsibility You Alone Are Responsible For The Way Your Life Is Placed Currently

Responsibility & Ownership are the two empowering words which when owned and adopted by you always strengthen you by revealing a clear road map for your success in life, making your dreams come true.

Destiny on the other hand in contrast is only a negative and consoling word used by timid defeatists in life which always DISEMPOWERS THEM.

Defeatists unfortunately are merely content fooling themselves by finding excuses and hiding behind them to justify their own failures in life.

Therefore Please Take Responsibility.

Believe In Yourself.

This alone will make you totally unstoppable to reach your success, or any goal in your life ahead.

Once you take true ownership and have the patience and wisdom not to throw your hands up – similar to a coin dropping into a coin machine and the clutch will open the door or deliver the material you choose to get.

Conscious & responsibly owned decisions to design trajectories of your lives to your own desires and goals will enable your dreams to come true. You also enjoy the pleasure of feeling and watching the positive effects and results of your self-ordained thoughtful actions at every stage as a highly rewarding experience.

The quality and position with which we lead our lives is always determined by the power we can generate within ourselves to respond to the varied complex situations that we all encounter.

Once you accept your own responsibility for the way you are

now, it will be possible to transform and improve and convert the greatest adversity in your life to your advantage.

The wealth of life lies only in how you have allowed your experiences to enrich you no matter how small and trivial they may be.

Even Filth can generate the fragrance of beautiful Flowers.

Even Manure can transform itself into the sweetness of a Mango.

Assuming responsibility however, will also put you in the position of the driver's seat of your life empowering you to decide the nature and the volume of actions you wish to undertake from stage to stage.

True magic and success will undoubtedly unfold in your lives ahead, if you decide that you alone are responsible for the way your life is placed currently.

By this Affirmation, you will soon yourself develop the ability to respond positively and everything will start falling in place.

This Is Not Philosophical.

This Alone And Only Is The True Reality of Life!

Mantra 7

Destiny V/S responsibility & Ownership

Why Successful People Design Their Own Destiny

Destiny V/S Responsibility & Ownership Why Successful People Design Their Own Destiny.

Please appreciate Destiny is only a negative and consoling word which always DISEMPOWERS THE TIMID DEFEATISTS who are content finding excuses to hide their failures in life.

Responsibility & Ownership on the other hand and in contrast are empowering words which when practiced clearly always reveal the route and road map for your success.

To make your dreams come true, the first step is to stop fooling and consoling yourself by imagining being a victim of your destiny and playing the blame game. Become instead a master and an architect of your own destiny by taking things and actions in your own hands. For an example -

If your stomach is empty and starving,

If your child is crying of hunger,

Will you leave it to mere fate or divine will?

No – You will instead immediately take things in your own hands and find your solution – Won't you?

Consequently, it is simple logic for anyone to understand that whenever we are confronted with a real challenge in our lives, we have no option but to tackle the problem by taking it into our own hands.

Unfortunately however a convenient word called destiny has somehow become an easy escape route – to hide the failures of fatalists and provide a ruse and shield for their negativity and passivity instead of their owning up and taking responsibility with positivity.

Most failures content themselves playing the Blame Game.

In contrast to this ill-conceived and self-defeating passivity the successful people choose to become masters and architects of their own destiny and win in their lives ahead.

Mantra 8

Thinking Well Is Good, Planning Well Is Better Doing Well Is The Best of All

Thinking Well Is Good.
Planning Well Is Better.
Doing Well Is Best Of All.
(Through Dr. Kather M&J Wuppertal 1964)

Dr. Kattner explained with simple clarity that -

"You Will Never Do Well

Unless You Plan Well"

And You Can Never Plan Well Unless You Think Well.

Therefore before taking any task in hand, the first essential thing is to think, concentrate on thinking and then planning accordingly.

Confront your limits and expand your thoughts.

Well and only well planned strategies of today deliver results and successes of tomorrow."

What you focus on early in life,

Always shapes your future.

World class thinking and working by planning should be our goal.

Experiment this simple exercise with any simple thing you wish to achieve and you will be pleasantly surprised with the outcome.

If at any time your mind focuses on difficulties alone, try and train it to concentrate on the opportunities as well.

Your high expectations at work will become fulfilling realities when followed by commensurate higher efforts preceded by higher and deeper thinking.

Leaders do no magic, getting jobs done successfully – they do it only by thinking well at the very first step.

Solid thinking within a team, attracting thoughts from all the members well before final planning leads to consistent well performance. This is not by mere chance, luck or any trick. But it is achieved by combined efforts.

Deep thinking and planning only confronts to expand a reputation within the family, in the society which you belong to and in the business you are engaged in.

I pleasantly realized that such a clear German way of thinking and explaining made this simple and the most essential fact of life most clearly achievable making you most successful in achieving your objectives and goals in life.

Mantra 9

Thoughts – Words – Actions & Your Karmas In Life

Watch Your Thoughts – They Become Your Words

Watch Your Words – They Become Your Actions

Watch Your Actions – They Become Your Habits

Thoughts – Words – Actions & Your Karmas In Life.
Watch Your Thoughts – They Become Your Words.
Watch Your Words – They Become Your Actions.
Watch Your Actions – They Become Your Habits.

Words not only hold meaning but they also hold their own special kind of magical power to help you come over your challenges in life to achieve success.

An entrepreneur is essentially a visualizer and habitually an organizer of his thoughts, words and actions. This is required to make his vision acquire the shape as desired by him.

Your thoughts can create magic and everything you have ever wanted you can create.

Today's Thoughts Build Tomorrow's Dreams.

It is universally recognized that

"I Create By The Words I Speak."

Great Dreams Create Good Thoughts

Good Thoughts Precede Great Deeds

Great Deeds Precede Great Success.

Dreams and Thoughts must be churned repeatedly in our minds along with the goal we have decided to accomplish in lives.

Our Dreams, Wishes, Thoughts and Feelings are very important because they get into our subconscious from where they certainly manifest.

Our old Shastras (sacred texts) have for ages understood and preached the power of Words of Wisdom i.e. our Mantras which are not just for communication but also for major healing purposes.

Words turn into Beliefs – Wishes – Actions & Prayers to help healing.

Words are like keys – if you choose them right, they can open any heart and shut any mouth.

It takes normally for a child almost two years to learn to speak.

However, it takes a lifetime for grown-ups to learn what not to speak.

Speak Good Words

Think Good Thoughts

Do Good Deeds

Keep Your Circle Positive

What Goes Around

Comes Back Around

Be positive thinking,

Emit love and gratitude only,

Banish negative feelings whatsoever from your life.

Floods Gates of Accomplishment of all your wishes will open in your favour.

Mantra 10

Lack Of Resources Always Make You More Resourceful

Lack Of Resources Always Make You More Resourceful

My own childhood situation and circumstances having been completely uprooted from our ancestral Haveli and comforts during the partition of India in 1947, followed by a challenging childhood and a tougher life with minimal resources for years taught me a lesson -

To face challenges and difficulties boldly.

It has helped in shaping not only my own future and that of my immediate family and extended family, that of my colleagues and co-workers today. Also contributing to cost effective import substitution and Make in India reality in our own country which needs to be boosted further even today.

In a Tata Macgraw Hills Book written by the learned man Mr. Srivas Pandit on 20 Thought Leaders on the Indian Horizon after Independence they chose me as one among them.

Appreciating very much how an IITian like me could step by step raise an impeccable Indian company in a highly specialized field at par with mighty multinationals despite a meager initial startup capital of hardly Rs.10,000/- the eminent writer chose and attributed the undermentioned heading for the chapter focused on me reading as:

"Lack of Resources

Make you More Resourceful."

Mantra 11

Opportunities Come Knocking At Our Doors Throughout our Lives

Wise-Men Only Recognize & Encash them

Opportunities Come Knocking At Our Doors Throughout Our Lives Wisemen Only Recognise & Encash Them.

Life is not about counting how many chances you had. It is about how many chances you could capitalize in your life.

Opportunities keep knocking at our doors throughout our lives.

Most people treat them as mere noise. Wise people recognize and encash them.

Opportunities are always under our feet. We don't have to go anywhere. All we need to do is recognize them.

When people don't know how to recognize an opportunity, they complain of noise when it knocks.

The same opportunity never knocks twice. The next one may be better or worse, but it is never the same one.

Sometimes we feel all doors are closed in our life. But all the closed doors may not be locked, they may be waiting for your own knock to open.

Opportunities are never lost–they are always taken by other people who are ready and are thinking positive.

DAVID AND GOLIATH

We all know the story of David and Goliath. There was a giant who for ages was bullying and harassing the children in a German village.

One fine day, a 17-year-old shepherd by the name of David came to visit his cousins and asked "Why don't you stand up and fight the giant? The cousins were terrified and they replied, don't you see he is too big to hit.

But David said "No he is not too big to hit, he is too big to miss the opportunity of hitting and killing the giant forever.

The rest is history. We all know what happened. David killed the giant with a sling.

Same giant, but different perception.

Recognizing opportunity, not fear and danger.

A great thinker was asked, 'What is the meaning of life?'

He replied, ***'LIFE itself has no meaning, it's an Opportunity to create a Meaning'***.

Adversities in all forms do breed opportunity.

Mantra 12

Well Planned Strategies Of Today Deliver Results Tomorrow - Every Great Tree Was A Once A Small Seed

Well Planned Strategies Of Today Deliver Results Tomorrow - Every Great Tree Was A Once A Small Seed.

Well thought and planned strategies of today deliver success and results tomorrow.

The day you plant the seed is not the day you can eat the fruit.

Every great Oak that stood its ground was once a nut.

What you focus earlier in life – always shapes your future.

A 1000 Mile long race is always run using the first step forward.

Do not wait for things to happen–make them happen.

Mantra 13

LEARN TO ADJUST & ADAPT ALL YOUR LIFE

LIKE THE GREAT GANGES HAS DONE OVER THE AGES

Learn To Adjust & Adapt All Your Life Like The Great Ganges Has Done Over The Ages.

The great Ganges starts her journey from Gaumukh in the Himalayan mountain range. It transcends into plains making her way through the hard rocks, tough terrain and then travels to the sea integrating all alterations it has to make on route.

Midway for her, so many smaller water bodies merge into Ganga making it more mighty and majestic.

The river keeps on adjusting her course, cutting way through the plains and rocks alike... accepting changes in her path or provisions that are offered. In her culmination it transforms into an enormous river before merging into the Bay of Bengal.

Such adaptive quality makes it The Ganga – one of the most massive and revered rivers of our planet.

This is a lesson that all of us can learn from Mother Nature and from Ganga Maa.

Remember that bottlenecks and blockages will appear. But they have to be surpassed and surmounted by thinking and finding adjustments wherever necessary by flowing through slowly.

Adapting or altering according to the situations is absolutely normal and natural. It is nothing but fine-tuning your thinking and working capacities.

Mantra 14

"GENAUIGKEIT"

PERFECTION SHRESHTATHA. WHAT IS PERFECTION – WHY & HOW PERFECTION

"Genauigkeit"
Perfection Shreshtatha
What Is Perfection
Why Perfection
How Perfection.

57 Years ago in 1962 at the age of 22 when I entered my office at the Research & Development Wing of "M&J Fanal" at Wuppertal in Germany, the first thing I noticed engraved in golden letters on the wall was :

Genauigkeit (Meaning Perfection)

Small and Consistent Small Steps Only

Lead to Perfection.

Perfection However

Mind You – is Not a Small Thing!

The Germans who are reputed all over the world for their perfection had realized the immense significance of this simple statement and inscribed it boldly at the fore front of their entrance.

It is wrong to imagine that perfection can only be achieved by some most expansive, 'beyond the common's reach' investments and/or action.

Perfection comes only by our persistent, dedicated simple efforts and actions not only in our outcomes but overall in all aspects of our lives.

Precisely as they say "If you take care of small things first, the big things will take care of themselves automatically".

Perfection is not only a requirement of the products that we manufacture and use. Perfection must be attempted and achieved in all aspects of our attitude and behavior in lives thereby generating a sense of happiness, contentment and accomplishment, which is the real purpose of life.

Mantra 15

'Ekla Chalo'

When Situation Demands We Must Always Trust Our Own Inner Intuition and Rise in Life

'Ekla Chalo'
When Situation Demands We Must Always Trust Our Own Inner Intuition and rise in life

We all without exception – I repeat without exception, we all have within us an incredible inner guidance tool. And that is our intuition.

This Intuition we must use to our own good.

For this you need to leave enough room for yourself to feel and think within yourself.

Once you have clearly determined and made up your mind to achieve a well-chosen goal in your life, you can even tell most politely all your advisors or even family members if any, to leave you alone and not to disturb you for some time.

We must recognize always that answers to most of our questions are already there well within ourselves.

All we need is to sharpen our own thinking power to be able to search our own intuition.

The more centered and tuned we are within ourselves, the mightier and more successful we will grow.

If others do not trust your well thought and planned decision, never mind.

Do it alone – Ekla Chalo (means move alone).

This is precisely what I myself did in 1965-66.

Resigning from my lucrative job in Germany to return home and start from the scratch – much against the repeated advice of all my German colleagues and my boss there.

Most of them warned me that you will not be able to complete with industry giants and you will ultimately submit and perish.

However the Dream and the Desire already developed in myself were so strong that I felt convinced. I had already gained the requisite knowledge and experience in Germany showing me the direction to return home and start to accomplish my ultimate dream.

Consequently, once I decided Ekla Chalo and became totally committed & determined to pursue my logical dream to start alone all by myself one fine day. Look where I could reach by the dint of my own intuition.

Aided duly by the blessings of the Lord, my Revered Parents and the worthy team of my colleagues I was able to generate over the months and years thereafter a company and a product range of worldwide repute.

Mantra 16

SETTING YOUR GOALS AIMS & TARGETS

ARE A MUST TO GENERATE SUCCESS - DREAM BIG

Setting Your Goals Aims & Targets Are A Must To Generate Success - Dream Big.

Goals, Aims & Targets are a must to generate Drive, Passion and Enthusiasm in your life. This is what keeps us moving forward all the time.

Imagine playing a Foot Ball match without any goal posts would indeed be frustrating.

The greatest danger for most of us lie not in setting our aims too high and falling short – but in setting our aims too low and reaching the mark.

How unfortunate it is when people work to survive rather than thrive.

When you aim at the sky – you may hit a tree but if you aim as low as a tree, you may only hit the ground.

Always dream big yet start with small steps but in the direction of a greater aim.

Remember nothing great (even Rome) was built overnight. However, Rome was dreamt and conceived BIG.

So was and today is our C&S Electric Ltd. Despite our tiny start in the Garage, we had dreamt big from day one and have continued to raise our performance bars every year as we continue to dream bigger and bigger.

Mantra 17

Winners Never Quit & Quitters Never Win

Remember You Are Not Born A Winner – You Are Not Born A Loser You are Born A Chooser

Winners Never Quit & Quitters Never Win
Remember You Are Not Born A Winner – You Are Not Born A Loser You Are Born A Chooser.

We can Survive and Age
Or we can Live and Sparkle
Choice is Your Own.

This is also a well known and well tried Mantra.

Losers Want Security and Winners Seek Opportunity.

Never say die.

Never give up.

Setbacks are to be utilized to learn by preparing to get it right next time.

Life can sometimes be queer with its twists and turns, yet many failures do turn-about also. Winners always stick to the challenge and try again changing their approach not their goal.

Try and Fail is much better than Fail to Try.

Don't give up even if the pace seems slow. You will succeed with another step sooner than later.

Positive people may also have negative thoughts – but they are wise enough not to let such thoughts grow and destroy them.

Adversity serves as a masked opportunity. It is a never-before learning experience. All you have to do is see it this way.

The secret mantra is finding out positive in each negative. How to achieve this?

Difficult times and obstacles are sometimes a blessing in disguise signaling you to rise above the stated lines.

"I don't know how my story ends but nowhere in my text will it ever read – I gave up!"said our worthy past President Dr. Abdul Kalam.

Mantra 18

Human Beings Are Your Most Important Asset

Training & Skill Building Brings Optimum Results

Human Beings Are Your Most Important Asset Training & Skill Building Brings Optimum Results.

How 1% Genius & 99% untrained Geniasses cannot achieve what 1% Genius & 99% otherwise trained Geniasses can easily achieve. How the wise Germans cleverly developed standardization to achieve this?

From my part-time Management classes in 1964 in Wuppertal Germany, our Prof. Mueller used to explain with a fair bit of passion, but jokingly though that in the population of all countries as also in Germany, there is usually and hardly 1% Genius and 99% otherwise which he jokingly termed as Geni-asses.

The wise Genius in Germany, after a great deal of focused thinking devised the DIN STANDARDS for all imaginable Technical, Construction, Medical, Accounting and Non-Technical fields of activity in a simple and clear well-defined manner.

All drawings and dossiers and manuals produced by German Institutions in each and every part of their country would follow the same DIN Standard pattern.

Framed after years of constructive thinking, consequently even the 99% so called Geni-asses who were following these clearly defined Directions & Standards, would never go wrong in understanding them. They would thus always perform and produce like the Genius themselves would have liked them to do.

Resultantly, 1% Genius Inspiration and 99% well directed perspiration using simple disciplined hard work brought about the Great German Renaissance and Economic Growth after the vast destruction caused in the country during World War II.

Such standardization and the great Renaissance of the German Industry I have personally participated in and witnessed, a lesson which the entire world including (most importantly) our

India should learn, emulate and replicate speedily throughout her length and breadth.

Rigorous training is most essential for a future entrepreneur who has the will to do something creative. It also forms the most vital part of one's personal grooming making you stronger and more resolute to reach your summit.

Human Beings, we must understand are, "the most valuable Assets or Liabilities for any Company or any Country or Team.

Men who report to YOU are as Good as you make them or as Bad as you let them be!"

The common factor of responsibility is therefore always OURS– as the Leaders who succeed or fail to enthuse their teams and themselves to succeed.

Let us analyze all problems and issues and train ourselves and our associates. And keep training further from time to time to catch up with the changing world at large and farther beyond.

Success Is Failure Turned Inside Out.

Success Is The Silver Streak Of All Dark Clouds.

Mantra 19

What Cannot Be Cured Must Be Endured

Without Much Fuss However

What Cannot Be Cured Must Be Endured Without Much Fuss However.

Even the Bible includes an import a prayer such as:

God grant me the power to change and correct all wrong things. Grant me the serenity to accept things I cannot change, grant me the wisdom to know the difference.

Great German composer Ludwig Van Beethoven was in his late 20's when his hearing began to deteriorate. He was almost completely deaf by the final decade of his life.

He decided to accept and endure it and continued with his creative Compositions.

Had he been worrying and fretting over his impediments he could never have risen to the heights which he reached by enduring his handicaps.

As the old English proverb says, 'What cannot be changed for reasons beyond your control you must grin and bear it'.

Mantra 20

The 'Impossible' Is Nothing

But An Assumed And Untried Possible

The 'Impossible' Is Nothing But An Assumed And Untried Possible.

The Impossible is often an assumed and untried Possible only.

Try tackling your 'Impossible' with the 'I am Possible' approach and you will see that it works out.

Impossible–is a strange word, full of restrictions and mental hampering.

But why allow it to have such an impact over your progress?

History is full of examples on how by rejecting the one word 'impossible' propositions one can explore and succeed in finding out the 'possible' ways to succeed.

I will again repeat here that sometimes all doors may seem to be closed. But all those closed doors may not be locked – they may be waiting for your knock!

When someone says impossible, seize the challenge – Everything Is Possible – you just have to find how.

Impossible is an illusion which steals away your creativity.

Mantra 21

When The Going Gets Tough

The Tough Get Going

When The Going Gets Tough The Tough Get Going.

Tough Times Never Last,

Tough People With Positive Attitude Do!

They rise to the occasion to overcome their difficulties.

If you lose the conviction, you were never tough enough.

Turbulent times have always built great Leaders in the World.

There was a man who came from one of the poorest families in USA:-

- He failed in business at the age of 21,
- He was defeated in a legislative race at the age 22,
- He failed again in business at 26,
- He had a nervous breakdown at 27,
- He lost a congressional race at 34,
- He lost a senatorial race at 45,
- He failed in his effort to become the Vice-President of his nation at 47,
- He lost another senatorial race at age 49,

And finally he was elected as The President of United States of America at the age of 52.

This man was Abraham Lincoln.

To him defeat was a detour, not a dead end.

Your resolve to overcome your hardships and hindrances need to be tougher than the situations you face.

He decided to be tougher than the situations he faced. Today he is acknowledged as one of the most read and admired ideologists of the World.

Life they say is all froth and bubble. Only two things stand out -

a) Rock solid courage in your own challenges
b) Convictions and compassion with others during their challenges.

One must learn to never say die!

When things go wrong, as sometimes they will

When the road you are trudging seems all uphill

When the funds are low and the debts are high,

And you want to smile but you have to sigh,

When care is pressing you down a bit –

Rest if you must, but don't you quit.

Don't give up though the pace seems slow –

You may succeed with another blow.

Success is failure turned inside out

The sliver tint of the clouds of doubt,

And you never can tell how close you are,

It may be near when it seems so far

So stick to the fight when you're hardest hit

It's when things seem worst that you must not quit.

Difficult Times show what you are made up of when you contain them.

Mantra 22

Attitude Is The Foundation of a Man

Make It Possitive

Attitude Is The Foundation of a Man Make It Possitive.

Attitude My Dear Readers is the foundation of a Man.

The Empire State Building has successfully withstood all rough weather conditions and even earth quakes over a hundred years without any damage.

Why? Because the foundation is so strong.

Success and Failure is caused more by mental attitude than capabilities or conditions. One has to search for solutions, not the problems.

A happy person is not one with favourable circumstances, but one with a favourable attitude.

Every positive thought is a silent prayer which will change your Life.

Right attitude will never take you to the wrong direction.

If you can't be a pencil to write someone's happiness, then try to be a nice eraser to remove their sadness.

A negative mind will never give you a positive life.

Build a more and more positive attitude within yourself.

Develop an attitude of gratitude.

Attitude is everything. Life is 10% of what happens to you & 90% how you react to it.

Remember most of your stress comes from the way you respond, not the way life is. Adjust your attitude and you will see that all that extra stress is gone.

It is your Attitude

And not your Aptitude

Which determines and delivers your Altitude

In life.

Mantra 23

The Great Importance In Life Of Emotional Quotient Vs Intelligence Quotient

The Great Importance In Life Of Emotional Quotient Vs Intelligence Quotient.

Intelligence quotient generally refers to establish how intelligent we are. But how far and high can the Intelligence Quotient (IQ) take us to succeed in life?

Often one notices very intelligent people not succeeding much in life, when for instance they cannot get along with others in a team or an office or a factory. This is because they lack social and inter personal skills.

Emotional Quotient (EQ) measures the ability to comprehended and control our emotion in a positive and productive way. It can be achieved through self-awareness, self-management, self and other's motivation, empathy for others and social skills. You need to handle matters in a decent and conducive manner to create a happy and agreeable environment around you to maximize a positive output.

IQ may help guarantee success in examinations.

EQ guarantees success in life.

Mantra 24

Express Your Gratitude And Count Your Blessings Every Morning

Express Your Gratitude And Count Your Blessings Every Morning.

The power of gratitude stands above most of other teachings in life.

Gratitude is undoubtedly the magical way to bring more and more into your life!

Many people spend their lives in a relative scarcity merely because of the lack of gratitude in their attitudes.

Be careful not letting your pride and ego come in the way of your expressing gratitude.

If you wish to bring a turn-around in your life, the first thing is to make a list of things to be grateful for.

Believe it for sure that gratitude alone brings your whole mind into close harmony with creative energies of the universe.

This will shift your minds from the complaints and grudges you may have had and your expression of gratitude will bring in a totally different, positive direction in your life.

Gratitude

Start being grateful for all things that you feel good about.

Ungrateful thoughts of Jealousy, resentment, dissatisfaction or feeling of not having enough – these can never bring you what you want.

It is so because the negative thoughts emit negative emotions and will never succeed in bringing more into your life.

Expression of gratitude should also become the most powerful exercise for you.

You can start with saying thank you to God every morning as you get up.

The Daily practice of gratitude is one of the conduits by which your wish and wealth will come more easily to you when combined with your own sincere efforts.

Giving thanks and expressing gratitude for what you already have, turbo-charges your desire and sends a more powerful signal in the Universe to bring success to your dedicated efforts and accomplishment to your dreams.

Let the expression of gratitude become a definite part of your lives if you wish to become a successful individual.

Mantra 25

Success Is A Journey, Not The Destination

Importance of Success & Failure In Life

Success Is A Journey, Not The Destination. Importance of Success & Failure In Life

Success, is always a journey – not the destination. Success in reaching your goals is like reaching a rainbow.

The closer we go to a rainbow, the farther it recedes. The journey of success continues just like you keep chasing the rainbow.

Successful people and companies celebrate and pat their backs on their successes from time to time but they still continue to strive on and on for newer horizons otherwise they will stagnate.

A Journey to success entails continuous progress. Progress is a segment of the trek, not the end of it. It is the on-route appraisal of your journey towards the destination.

There is no elevator to success.

You have to take the stairs – Step by Step.

Importance of Success & Failure In Life.

SUCCESS will never lower its Standard to accommodate us. It is we who have to raise our standards to achieve it.

Success & Failure in Life

Success or Failure in business is always caused more and more by mental attitudes, than by mental capabilities or external conditions. Discovering excuses never helps.

Our Attitude determines how we look at a setback.

To a positive thinker, it can be a stepping stone to success.

To a negative thinker, it can be a stumbling block.

Every success story is also a story of a great failure.

Failure is the highway to success. The Great Philosopher Tom Watson Sr. said, "If you want to succeed, double your failure rate."

If you study history, you will find that all stories of success are also stories of great failure.

But people do not see the failures. They only see one side of the picture and they say that person got lucky, 'He must have been at the right place at the right time.'

Success introduces you to the World,

But Failure introduces the World to you.

Always ask yourself after every failure or setback: What did I learn from this experience?

Only then will you be able to turn a stumbling block into a stepping stone.

Success is the sum of small efforts repeated day in and day out.

Life is in some ways similar to a Boxing Game...

Defeat or failure is NOT declared when you fall down;

It is declared when you refuse to 'GET UP'.

So what if you have failed in the past,

So what if you may fail again,

You are not the only one who failed.

Every successful human being also failed but tried again and again and so can you as explained in this book.

Most great men have also failed at multiple times in their lives but they never gave up trying again.

Abraham Lincoln the Great American President was only a poor farmer's son looking after a pig sty in the farm where he was born. He struggled hard and failed time and again but never gave up and rose to become one of the most respected Presidents of the U.S.A.

Our Own Great Prime Minister Sh. Narender Modi before transforming our Country and regaining our Country's lost glory, was merely selling tea on the railway stations earlier when his life began.

How hard he worked climbing the ladders of success and failure are well known already.

Step by step they all climbed to their glories ultimately–so can you.

We must recognize that for them their failures were always considered as their challenges and stepping stones to their greater success ladders in history.

Success is neither magical nor mysterious. Success is the natural consequence of good and positive habits and actions alone.

Mantra 26

Men Who Work For You Are As Good As You Make Them Or As Bad As You Let Them Be

Men Who Work For You Are As Good As You Make Them Or As Bad As You Let Them Be.

Your team is your most valuable asset.

Men who report to you are as good as you make them or as bad as you let them be - the responsibility stays with you.

Abrahim Lincoln used to say-

"Ten men bonded together enthused and motivated together in a team – can achieve what 10000 unenthused and unmotivated in one direction individually cannot."

A motivated and enthused team is the greatest asset of any organization.

As a leader of your home team, your resident welfare society, your company or your country – the leader has to play a very important role in making great organizations work.

Mr. Sridharan is considered as one of the greatest Indian Leaders in the Management of Infrastructure Projects. Konkan Railways and the Delhi Metro are two living examples of his successful team work. And that of intelligently choosing the right kind of people and delegating them to work supporting each other towards achieving the end goal. That was Mr. Sridharan's specialization.

Good individuals and specialists are important for any organization but only if they can be motivated to work with utmost Team Spirit.

The individual skills of your team members must complement each other.

We must realize that the sum total of the performance of a team is much larger than the sum total of the output of each member.

Likewise it is also important to understand with absolute clarity that men who report to you are as good as you make and empower them, and are as bad as you let them be.

The responsibility stays always with the leader.

The major Mantras of team building to keep people around you motivated can be seen as below -

Trust–That each one of us need each other

Gratitude–It is a choice every leader should choose, because a thankful heart is a happy heart

Honest communication

Sharing of responsibility

The Team Leader's ability to shed or nurture self-ego, maturity and patience in behavior, systematic team building and building up of team spirit should be the first and foremost area of attention for any leader.

And it goes true everywhere – whether it is the workplace, sports ground, home or relations.

Because effective team building induces that extra zeal, that extra energy and will-power into the minds of people striving for a common cause, which is their organization's success.

The simple Word Team can be remembered for ease to understand as follows:

TEAM

T for Together

E for Each One

A for Achieves

M for More

Together Each One Achieves More.

Mantra 27

IF YOU HAVE A BETTER IDEA AND I HAVE ONE

WHEN WE SHARE THEM

WE CAN HAVE TWO GOOD IDEAS EACH

If You Have A Better Idea And I Have One
When We Share Them
We Can Have Two Good Ideas Each.

Sharing brings peace and harmony in organizations.

Good ideas and constructive suggestions must be passed and shared in a family, in a team, in a company and this holds the key to effective coordination in any enterprise. Such coordination can be achieved through continuous sharing of thoughts between all the people shouldering a common responsibility–regardless of their hierarchical position in the company.

If you decide to carry on your own ideas all by yourself by being secretive, you invite to yourself a high risk of vulnerability.

The workability of an idea, its execution and profitability need to be checked upon before implementation. You may have checked it all by yourself, but in the absence of a second opinion the end results can surprise you.

Without sharing your ideas, it can expose you to grave dangers rather than credits!

But when you share the idea with your team, you have the ease and liberty to work on it more aptly and adeptly – thereby minimizing the risks involved.

In addition, this also opens the gates for your team to come to you whenever they have a fruitful brainwave – an understanding that culminates in a faster and better success all around.

Mantra 28

Where Ego Fills The Space
Progress Loses Its Pace

Where Ego Fills The Space
Progress Loses Its Pace.

Ego and Love are branches of the same tree. Just that the difference is,

Love always wants to say sorry,

And ego always wants to hear it.

Ego is a small three letter word,

Which can destroy a big twelve letter word called Relationship.

If ego expands to fill space then the mind cannot sustain perception. Staying away from ego hassles and being receptive is essential in Life.

Successful Entrepreneurs & Leaders must unconditionally shed their own egos if any.

Select and employ even more qualified specialists in respective field, however with positive attitudes.

Learn and understand from these specialists and then with your own positive attitude and approach. Guide and motivate such specialists towards the company's vision to ensure optimum and accelerated success results.

A rather famous example from recent times can explain this fact.

In the year 2006 when the automobile giant Ford was struggling to regain its business, a senior executive Mark Fields, the Strategy Incharge famously went on to admit his strategical failure in a high-level executive meeting.

This was absolutely unheard of at Ford, and the crew present wasn't sure of fate of Mark as well as the company after this confession.

But the newly appointed CEO, Alan Mulally surprisingly for all, applauded Mark in one of the most highly visible moment at the organization.

This changed the way the company operated and marked the beginning of a turn-around for Ford.

What did the trick is the fact that this particular incident set the tone open for a new culture of honest communication and confessions at its offices. It was an ego-free environment now.

Burn your ego

Before it burns you.

Ego is a double edged sword.

The outer edge slashes your popularity while the inner edge slashes your purity.

While Mark introduced this truthfulness into operating systems setting aside his ego hang-ups, Alan had emboldened his frankness.

This brought about a much-needed change in the way the enterprise earlier performed under his predecessors.

Mark eventually went on to succeed Alan as the next top boss at Ford.

How important it is to stay away from ego for an organization or individual's multi-dimensional growth!

Mantra 29

The Need To Develop Ownership Mentality And Attitude In Your Team For A Well-knit & Well Performing Organization

The Need To Develop Ownership Mentality And Attitude In Your Team For A Well-knit & Well Performing Organization.

Good and Creative Managements should try to create a culture of personal accountability and encourage their employees to possess a total ownership attitude in their areas of operation.

It is one of the most important, powerful and desired characteristics of a successful organization.

Listening to employees on frequent intervals through formal forums or even at informal occasions like a birthday bash or a chat during lunch hour and then acting on those inputs can help in cultivating 'Ownership Mentality' in the minds of the employees.

The Mantra of Ownership Mentality Attitude will set you apart from the average employees in the organization and finally put you on a pedestal much higher than your counterparts.

For employees who start thinking and contributing like being the owner of the business wherever they are, chances are that one day they will actually become senior officials and CEOs in a real sense.

Start investing your time and efforts in improving your performance and deliverables as if you own the business. It does not cost anything yet it reaps healthy dividends sooner than later.

Start learning more and more about the organization and about what you do. Be innovative in your approach and be proactive in the meetings to suggest ways on how the company can expand and increase its quality and profits.

If you sincerely see a wastage or something wrong anywhere in the company, be bold enough to point out and suggest a remedy.

With this approach, you are bound to get noticed and rightly so by the top management. This will pave the path for your personal and professional growth and promotions up the leadership ladder will follow.

Good and far sighted owners should also always encourage such a responsible attitude of the employees and come out willingly with suitable promotions and rewards to encourage more and more such Employees.

Such a positive approach does a lot of good both to the management and to the employees in a win-win situation manner and a pleasure is felt in working together.

Mantra 30

WE CAN DO IT
WE SHALL DO IT
WE WILL DO IT

We Can Do It!
We Shall Do It!
We Will Do It!

Our own in-house developed slogan that we repeated together at our Annual Founders Day Celebrations.

A very famous incident from the pages of history can explain this best.

When Alexander the Great arrived on the shores of Persia his army was heavily outnumbered by the Persians. Yet he gave strict orders to his men to burn all their own boats in which they had come ashore. They had to actually 'Burn' their wooden boats following his orders.

Alexander did so for a very good reason. With their only means to retreat going up in flames his men were left without a choice but to win! This made their fear vanish... for now they had to fight for their own survival.

Alexander is known to have turned to his men and announced, "We go home in Persian ships, or we perish." What followed was an astounding victory they secured over an army which was superior to theirs in many ways.

Because for them, it was win or die...simple.

Such is the power of a will to succeed.

New Zealand Captain Cook in New Zealand did the same and that is how New Zealand is what it is today.

And so did we in our C&S Electric one day by developing our own home raised slogan

We Can Do It – We Shall do it – We will Do it!

This had a magical effect on our Indigenization & Development Team.

We had been compelled to indigenize and locally produce intricate components for our Air Break Contactors and

Switchgear at a stage when our former joint venture Collaborators Telemecanique of France imposed an unfortunate unilateral temporary embargo on the supply of essential parts on account of some commercial misunderstandings hoping that we will fold up soon thereafter and handover the company to them.

I called for a closed door meeting with my Senior Managers from all divisions. After a detailed and lengthy analysis of the problem and the actions need to overcome this sudden hurdle, I requested my colleagues to recite and repeat three times together with me,

We can do it

We shall do it

We will do it.

We all tightened our belts and pooled in our efforts. All the required parts were locally produced matching up to the same quality as per our standards and norms. Resultantly not only we succeeded in meeting our delivery commitments, the heavy outflow of import duty costs were also saved.

The Company made excellent profits and progress in meeting our rising market demands, maintaining quality, delivery costs and customer service and Telemechanic also appreciated our initiative in this joint venture.

Ever since then on all our important Annual Yearly Founders Day Celebrations we all pool in together to recite three times this company slogan serving as a thundering reminder to what we can achieve when we resolve together as a team.

We can do it – We shall do it – We will do it
And we did do it!

Mantra 31

The Sweetest Reward Comes From The Hardest Struggle

The Sweetest Reward
Comes From The Hardest Struggle.

Honey Bees must tap two hundred flowers to make one drop of honey.

Remember that the sweetest reward comes from the hardest struggle.

"Even for cherry trees, it is said, if the period of winter chill required for breaking dormancy is Insufficient, the flowering of the buds will be delayed and the blossoms will be irregular.

The key to victory in our lives is how hard we struggle when we are in winter, how wisely we use that time and how meaningfully we will live each day confident that spring will definitely come...

Therefore we must not avoid the trials of winter."

However in order to succeed, we must first believe that we can.

You can't meet a Challenge without Change -

You have to be Ready for a Change,

If you wish to Rise to a Challenge in life.

Mantra 32

Strive For Newer Horizons

Otherwise You Will Stagnate

Strive For Newer Horizons Otherwise You Will Stagnate.

A leader and a manager for self, a company or a Country must know how to look beyond your targets - have a vision for the future.

Maintain the momentum. The moment you drop that compulsory velocity, you run the risk of falling back to zero.

Consider while driving uphill, one has to press the accelerator persistently – you loosen your grip on it and your vehicle starts receding immediately before coming to a halt. You end up a few yards even behind your starting point!

If you fail to conquer and usher in new techniques and methodologies you will not go too far in the race.

Because feeling safe

And experiencing zero adventure

Can crush your appetite to surge ahead.

In such a case you may end up staying in the same small pool with limited opportunities thereby making it insufficient to sustain your achievement. You will feel stagnated.

Do not let this happen to you.

Mantra 33

Happiness Is What We All Long For

However No Rainbow Without A Rain

Happiness Is What We All Long For However No Rainbow Without A Rain.

Everybody wants happiness, nobody wants pain. However we must clearly understand that there can't be a rainbow without a little rain.

Likewise happiness is not the absence of problems, it is the ability to deal with them. Happiness is the spiritual experience of living every minute with love, grace and gratitude.

Personal Internal Strength Is Happiness. Awakening Personal Internal Strength Is Itself A Victory.

In weakness and cowardice on the other hand there is no happiness. When you wage a struggle, you might win or you might lose. But regardless of the short-term outcome, the very fact of your continuing to struggle is proof of your victory as a human being. Being happy is to let live the individual that lives in each of us – free, joyful and simple.

It is to have maturity to be able to say, yes I made mistakes.

It is to have the courage to say I am sorry.

By such actions of ownership may your life become a garden of opportunities for nurturing happiness.

Use your Mistakes to Sculptor Serenity.

Use Pain to Plaster Pleasure.

Use Obstacles to Open Windows If Intelligence.

Never give up on people who love you.

Never give up on Happiness, for life is an incredible show.

Happiness you can undoubtedly generate with your positive attitude and simple understanding as explained above.

Focus on radiating a feeling of joy and happiness among your family members and your colleagues and you will be surprised! The Universe and the Nature will bring it back to you.

Mantra 34

Shun Anger And Bring Instead - Peace, Change & Confidence In Your Life

Shun Anger And Bring Instead - Peace, Change & Confidence In Your Life.

Anger/Patience - Peace & Change

A Saint was asked - "What is anger?"

He gave a beautiful answer -

"It is a punishment we give to ourselves, for somebody else's mistake."

Anger Resentment and Blame Game only leads to Deprivation effecting your own harm – mind you.

ANGER comes Alone.

But Takes Away all the Good Qualities from us.

PATIENCE too comes Alone.

But Brings all Good Qualities to us.

Choice is ours !!

Stay away from anger, it hurts only you.

If you are right, then there is no need to get angry.

And if you are wrong, then you don't have any right to get angry.

Patience with Family is Love

Patience with Others is Respect

Patience with Self is Confidence and

Patience with GOD is Faith.

There are times when the coolest people get angry. What is note-worthy is that they soon find ways to diffuse such a situation by taking wind off from the bloated anger of the person across so that he can willingly understand your message without brooding over it.

Peace

Peace does not mean to be in a place where there is no noise, no trouble or no hard work. It means, on the contrary, to be amid all of these and yet be calm in your mind and heart.

Anything that costs you your Peace is too expensive.

Your Life Becomes Masterpiece

When You Learn To Master Peace

Change

I asked a Monk, 'How to feel tall?'

He just Smiled and Bowed.

One reason people resist change is because they focus on what they have to give up–instead of focusing on what they have to gain.

Be Bold when you Lose

Be Calm when you Win

Changing the face can change Nothing.

But,

Facing the change can change Everything.

Mantra 35

Confident Walking Is Better Than Confused Running

Confident Walking Is Better Than Confused Running.

Confident walking is always better than confused running.

Follow no one, but learn from everyone.

Confidence doesn't come when you have all the answers...

Confidence essentially comes when you are ready to face all the Questions.

Self Confidence is an amazing super power. Once you start to believe in yourself, magic begins to show up.

For young ones who wish to start writing the story of your life,

Do not let anyone else hold the pen,

Gradually develop maturity and confidence in yourself and then,

Choose the life you wish ahead,

All by yourself.

An umbrella cannot stop the rain, but it can make us stand in the rain with confidence.

Confidence may not bring immediate success, but it certainly gives you the power to face any challenge in life leading to success.

Mantra 36

The Importance Of Prayer / Kindness / Relationship / Forgiveness

The Importance Of Prayer / Kindness / Relationship / Forgiveness.

Prayers dreams and seeds are similar in nature. They all have nothing within, but they have the potential to create everything.

Prayer is the first ever cordless phone that was created by God. He termed it 'Prayer'.

It never loses its signal and you never have to recharge it.

You can use it anywhere.

Kindness

If you have to choose between being kind and being right,

Choose being Kind and you will always be Right.

Relationship

A great relationship is about two things,

First - Find Out The Similarities

Second - Respect The Differences

Forgiveness

"Forgive Others Not Because They Deserve Forgiveness, But Because You Deserve Peace."

Simple principle of Life is:

No matter how many times teeth bite the tongue, they still stay and work together. Such is the spirit of forgiveness and relationship.

Having a sharp memory is a good quality of the brain. But the ability to forget the unwanted things is a far better quality of the heart.

Live In Peace, Not In Pieces.

Mantra 37

Grudges Must Be Shunned

Stay Away From Self Pity & Blame Game

Grudges Must Be Shunned
Stay Away From Self Pity & Blame Game.

People spend too much time in finding their lucky stars to win or to fix the blame on others and finding grudges or excuses for not having been able to do what they are capable of.

Blaming failures on hard luck or crediting success with good luck – it is a useless and negative thinking.

Remember That Luck Or Success Or Fate Shines On The Deserving Only.

Whenever you feel that being stuck in a given situation is a signal by the fate spelling your doom, be sure that it is your own negative thinking that is spelling the doom for you.

One of the most dangerous curves is the curvature of self-victimization. Because that is the easiest getaway from a problem of any sort!

I call it the curvature of self-victimization, as it is a part of a circle – a vicious circle which has no end.

Once you start moving along it you will end up going around and round endlessly, ceaselessly until you yourself choose to emerge out of it.

Do not ever, ever fall prey to self-pity.

Stop becoming a victim of self-pity and fate.

With a positive belief in your heart and mind enjoy reading this book to feel enthused and victorious soon again.

Life taught me not to complain about others, change yourself if you want peace.

Because it is easier to protect your feet with slippers than to carpet the whole world.

When you hold grudges, your hands aren't free to hold the blessings.

Mantra 38

Your Body Is Your Life Partner

No One Can Help Your Body Better Than You

Your Body Is Your Life Partner
No One Can Help Your Body Better Than You.

Who is your life partner?

Mom, Dad, Wife, Son, Husband, Daughter, Friends?

None at all!

Your Real Life Partner Is Your Own Body.

Once your body stops responding no one is there with you.

You are your body staying with you from Birth till Death.

What you do to your body is your responsibility and that only will come back to you.

The more you care for your body, the more the body will care for you.

What you Eat,

What you do for being Fit,

How you deal with Stress

How much Rest you give to it

Will decide how your body is going to respond.

Your body is your asset and/or your own liability, which no one else can share.

Your body is your responsibility.

And because of this, you are the Real Life Partners.

Remember your body is the only permanent address where you live.

Be Fit Forever

Take Care Of Yourself

Money Comes And Goes

Relatives And Friends Are Not Permanent

Remember That No One Can Help Your Body Other Than You.

Therefore:

Pranayama – For Lungs,
Meditation – For Mind,
Yoga-Asanas – For Body,
Walking – For Heart,
Good Food – For Intestines,
Good Thoughts – For Soul,
And Good Karma – For World.

Mantra 39

The Importance of Understanding

Patience / Impatience

Crisis/Fear

Risk/Danger

Silence & Smile

The Importance of Understanding

Patience / Impatience

Crisis/Fear

Risk/Danger

Silence & Smile.

Patience with Family is Love

Patience with Others is Respect

Patience with Self is Confidence

Patience with God is Faith

Patience is not about the ability to wait, but the ability to keep a good attitude while waiting.

Look at the way a farmer sows the crop, starting by surrendering a seed to the soil. Then he waters and guards the seed. He waits patiently till the time the seed is ready to show up as a tiny sapling. Then he carefully nurtures the little plant till it develops into a crop ready to bear fruits in a patient manner and he succeeds.

Learn to be patient like farmers –

Doing the right thing at just the right time.

Patience does not mean to endure passivity. It means to look at the end of a process.

Patience What does patience mean?

It means to look at the thorn and see the rose, to look at the night and see the dawn.

Impatience means to be short sighted as to not be able to see the outcome. The lovers of God never run out of patience, for they know that time is needed for the moon crescent to become full.

It is better to be melted in feelings than to be frozen in differences.

Crisis, Danger & Risk, Fear

Silence & Smile

Written in the Chinese language the word 'Crisis' is composed of two characters–one represents 'Danger', the other, 'Opportunity'.

Challenges are what make life Interesting.

Overcoming them is what makes life Meaningful.

You cannot stop trouble from coming, but you don't have to give it a chair to sit on.

FEAR has two meanings -

Forget Everything And Run

Or

Face Everything And Rise.

THE CHOICE IS YOURS.

Taking Calculated Risks is a Must

The objective of all good businesses or activity in life is a profit or a gain through taking calculated risks.

Those Who Cannot Shake The Dice,

Will Never Throw A Six.

Silence & Smile

Are two powerful words

Smile is the way to Solve many Problems

And Silence is the way to Avoid many Problems.

Mantra 40

Be Daring, Be Determined And Be Different For Quantum Success

Be Daring, Be Determined And Be Different For Quantum Success.

HAVE FAITH IN YOURSELF SHUN WORRY & FEAR

'Progress has always resulted for those who were bold enough to choose their unique and challenging paths. Not for those who go merely following the easier beaten tracks.'

Be Daring,

Be Different,

Align Your Thinking,

Dedicate Your Energies and then

You Can Achieve.

If you believe in yourself, others will believe in you.

Have faith–it does not make things easy, it makes them possible.

Both Faith and Fear might sail into your harbour.

But it's your harbor–and you decide who gets to drop anchor!

Worry Disturbs Mind

But

Prayer Releases Peace

Bring Peace Through Action and Prayer.

Reflection cannot be seen in the boiling water. Similarly, solution cannot be seen with a disturbed mind. So cool down and you will find solution for your problem.

Mantra 41

'Time' You Can Never Hold Borrow Or Generate - Only Spend

'Time' You Can Never Hold Borrow Or Generate - Only Spend

Time is one thing you can never hold borrow or generate– you can only spend waste or utilize it.

Time is almost flying so the only thing we can do is to manage our time well.

If you take care of your minutes, the hours will take care of themselves.

Every morning, you must develop a habit to write down a list of important things that need to be done that particular day.

Focus your attention to do them or delegate them being done so as to check before the end of the day their accomplishment.

If anything is not accomplished, let it go on to become the first one due on next day's list.

Anyone who does this simple thing religiously day by day is bound to emerge much more effective than his counter-parts in life.

Our Ancestors were wise people and they arranged to divide the 24 hours of a day in three equal parts.

The first 8 hours were for self–spread over say 6 hours of sleep and 2 hours of physical exercise, meditation and prayer.

The second lot of 8 hours was meant for dedicated hard work.

The third slot of 8 hours was meant for the family friends and society.

This was a great way to create an excellent work-life balance.

Life and time are world's two biggest teachers. Life teaches us to make good use of time. Time teaches us to take good care of our life.

Try your own best spread of time so as to utilize every minute of your life – as time is the most precious thing which nothing can buy.

Mantra 42

The Importance Of Parental & Family Strengths To Build Your First Foundations In Life

The Importance Of Parental & Family Strengths To Build Your First Foundations In Life.

Habit Of Early Rising & Advantages In Life

Parental & inherent family strengths always build our first own fundamental foundation to start our lives with.

Our parents always to a great extent shape us in our initial years.

My biggest motivation was the story my revered father read out to me and my elder brother Sati when I was hardly 8 years old. It was the story from a book by Dale Carnegie on how to stop worrying and succeed in life.

For years I kept on scribbling in my note books and repeating the under-mentioned lines read out and explained by my father, which later changed the course and purpose of my life –

"Heights by great men reached and kept were never attained by sudden flights – but they while their companions slept were toiling upwards in the skies."

All the while learning and remembering that I myself have to take the initiative to shape up my life and my future, this is what I exactly did.

Enormous joy, success and confidence is readily found in cultivating relationship within your own family, no matter how small or big it may be. So, never neglect your family.

A solid first foundation and initial relationship at home always initiates a strong and solid result oriented foundation at work also in later years.

Feeling cared for, appreciated and loved by your own family no matter how small it may be, is always such a powerful initial accelerator and catalyst for your leadership qualities and personal success. You thereby grow by leaps and bounds for much bigger pedestals later in life.

Early Rising

My father used to say –

Try to develop in yourself the great habit of rising early say by 5.30 to 6.00 AM or even earlier every morning. For most productive results great leaders of the world have all done so before.

The way you start your day will determine how well will you live it. I have said so and realized this all through my life.

Your first thoughts and hours set up how will you perform during the day.

Likewise, your last thoughts before sleep also have a big influence on what goes in between the morning and late evening.

My father said that if you sincerely tell yourself to rise early in the morning, your subconscious will wake you up. Till date I am used to this.

Do not ever let individual egos and jealousies burn and ruin your inherent family strength which will always assist you at all levels later in your life.

Mantra 43

The Most Desired 25 Leadership Kaizen How To Lead Well

The Most Desired 25 Leadership Kaizen How To Lead Well.

- Believe in the capabilities of the people you are leading.
- Maturity and patience – first and foremost qualities of a leader.
- Recall to your team with confidence, 'We can do it, We shall do it, We will do it'.
- Adopt and practice the age old rule–that of doing business with ethics.
- Good ideas and good products are 'Good' only if marketed and sold with planned strategies.
- Do not expect your subordinates to be exceptional unless you are exceptional.
- 'Ten men bonded and motivated together in a team can achieve what 10,000 individuals cannot.' Build motivated teams.
- Tough times never last, but tough people do. Rise to the occasion.
- Human beings are the most valuable assets or liabilities for any company – choose your men carefully.
- Anything or everything that we do should be a self-ordained, self-paralleled improvement from day to day. Then only the cumulative effect will be phenomenal.
- When one is pitched against the odds the way you see it can make all the difference. Lead from the front.
- Self-assessment of your efforts gives you the confidence to advance. For if you know how you are doing, then only it is wise to go the way you were.
- Your vision has to be statistical. Count and note your strengths and weaknesses carefully.
- Your vision has to be opaque–not to the dreams but to the bounties offered by those dreams. Only those who are

led by such wisdom and exactitude are the ones who can gather honey from the weeds.

- 'The fresh thinking that leads to a company's initial success is often replaced by a rigid devotion to the status quo.' Never do so.
- Think world class, transfer your thoughts to your team. Be open to sharing.
- Remember that money, inheritance and position is nothing as compared to empowered minds.
- Work ethics and principles are created, hired and imparted to let the organization shine and grow.
- **SSEW – Something Seriously Exceptional work** – always try do this. Play at your peak and the results will follow.
- Thinking of failure and accepting mediocrity amounts to surrendering the genius that was within you.
- A winner is already a winner even before he wins because he has worked hard to dedicate his thinking to creating greatness in whatever he undertakes.
- Be watchful of expenses and wastages however minute. A penny saved is a pound made. Even a small leak can sink a great ship.
- Evaluate the environment that we have created for ourselves and others.
- Real leadership involves breaking through the limits of your mind and stepping into the highest strengths of your spirits.
- As a boss, you may not be able to make your subordinates always deliver meatier results. But as long as you are able to make them genuinely wish they could have done better, your job is done.

Do Not Nurture Your Problems

Do not Live under the Burden of unsolved Problems

The Answer To A Problem Lies Hidden Within The Problem Itself.

If You Fail To Deal With Reality, Reality Will Have To Deal With You.

Certain facts and fractions are always there that you do not like dealing with – they may even be painful, but they've got to be tackled. Because it will be worth later on.

The key is to discover the solution to a problem and not just watch it coming – waiting for the consequence to come to you. A hurdle that surfaces as an obstacle in your path has to be confronted no matter how challenging it may appear.

I can suggest a simple exercise which may help you. Pick up a pen and paper, write down the problem. Now note down your sequential chain of thoughts.

Bring to the book even your assumptions, conclusions and the actions you took pertaining to that area.

Analyze and re-analyze your notes and you will surely see light.

Make a note on how and where you need to exercise the corrective remedy, if any.

Albert Einstein said he was successful because he spent more and more time analyzing the problems and finally found the solutions in them only.

Running away from any solvable problem only increases its distance from the solution.

The easiest way to escape from a problem is to solve it. Therefore, solve the problem or leave and uproot the problem from your mind forever.

Do not live under the burden of unsolved problems.

Follow the 'what cannot be cured must be endured' principle.

Remember that, A Problem Is Not Like Wine - It Does Not Get Better With Age.

It is like a weed which shall magnify if not uprooted in time.

Mantra 44

Wise Men Keep Learning All Their Lives

Leave Your Schooling Behind And Keep Learning

Wise Men Keep Learning All Their Lives - Leave Your Schooling Behind And Keep Learning.

Wise men leave their schooling behind, but continue learning all their lives.

Even age is only a state of your mind. Try and feel young enough to keep learning and enjoying yourself.

Learning is a continuity, an essential soft skill. One should develop it at all costs.

It can be acquired at any age from anywhere – in a classroom, or in a boardroom.

How often learning is confused with education which is in fact only an initial part of the complete learning process.

Wholesome learning is the acquisition of knowledge through three gradients –

Knowledge

Training and

Experience

Only then it becomes complete. It is after such composite process that we are able to develop a refined wisdom.

It helps us utilize the opportunities and the resources around us successfully. In absence of either of the three we remain susceptible to the threats and perils of entrepreneurial challenges.

If you are not open to learning you not only stop but you recede in your mental growth–mind you.

Tell Me and I Forget

Teach Me and I Remember

Involve Me and I Learn To Contribute

Such is the right approach in life.

Mantra 45

Heaven & Hell My Dear Readers Are Not Any Geographical Locations - You Can Create Your Own Heaven Yourself

Heaven & Hell My Dear Readers Are Not Any Geographical Locations - You Can Create Your Own Heaven Yourself.

Heaven & Hell Are In Reality And Always

Only THE OUTCOME of

Our Dreams Thoughts & Behaviour

Our Desires Directions & Commitment

Our Ownership & Responsibility Assertions

They are the outcome of all our consequent actions and exertions in dealing with challenges and opportunities we face in our lives.

Always feel free to identify your own specific dreams, passions and longings which you wish to achieve in your lives whatever they may be.

Start looking within yourself, by taking responsibility for harnessing your own energy that always exists in all of us human beings including you.

That tremendous internal energy within us, is waiting to be tapped and utilized for our own good to create our own heavens in our lives ahead.

Mantra 46

WORRYING IS A WASTEFUL EXERCISE, STOP WORRYING &

DEEPLY STUDY THE PROBLEM THE SOLUTION ALWAYS

LIES HIDDEN IN THE PROBLEM ITSELF

Worrying Is A Wasteful Exercise. Stop Worrying & Deeply Study The Problem, The Solution Always Lies Hidden In The Problem Itself.

Solution Always Lies Hidden in the Problems

Curiosity Is The Fuel for Success & For Motivation in Life

Curiosity is the Mother of Invention

Albert Einstein used to say, "Solution always lies well hidden in the problem."

The secret of his success was that he spent more and more time on focusing and studying the problem to explore the solution he always found hidden therein.

Do not give up the search for solution.

Curiosity

Being curious is a good sign, why?

Because curiosity alone can inspire our mind to find solutions to questions that fascinate us. It has a tremendous potential that ignites our motivation.

By definition Curiosity is a super exciting and extremely fertile sensitivity of human intellect that leads to discoveries.

Curiosity was how steam engine was engineered by James Watt. When James saw the lid of a utensil being pushed hard, his curiosity pushed him harder to look for a reason.

Curiosity initiates a potential to create, explore or discover.

Mantra 47

18 Signs Of Maturity How Mature You Are

18 Signs Of Maturity How Mature You Are.

Maturity is when you stop trying to change people and instead of focus on changing yourself.

Maturity is when somebody hurts you and you try to understand their situation instead of trying to hurt them back.

Maturity is when you accept people for who they are.

Maturity is when you understand that everyone is right in their own perspective.

Maturity is when you realize that nothing is more important in this world than you, your family and your extended family including colleagues.

Maturity is when you understand that whatever you do is for your own peace.

Maturity is when you stop proving to the world how intelligent you are.

Maturity is when you focus on positives in people.

Maturity is when you do not seek approval from others.

Maturity is when you stop comparing yourself to others.

Maturity is when you are at peace with yourself.

Maturity is when you can differentiate between need and want and you can let go of your wants.

Maturity is when you stop attaching happiness to material things.

Maturity is when you learn to let go, accept the situations and move on.

Maturity is when you do not react to the behavior of insane people.

Maturity is when one drops expectations from a relationship and gives for the sake of giving.

Maturity is learning to walk away from people and situations that threaten your peace of mind, self-respect, values, morals or self-worth.

Maturity is when you have a lot to say, but you choose to remain silent in front of fools.

Mantra 48

Temporarily Choosing A Role Model Is A Universally Tried Method, Discarding It When You Are Well On Your Road Likewise

Temporarily Choosing A Role Model Is A Universally Tried Method, Discarding It When You Are Well On Your Road Likewise.

Would You Like To Choose One?

To follow & visualize and emulate even if temporarily to discard the role model once after you are well on your road.

On the Basis of what you have read so far in this book beginning from the Prologue and Introductory Articles, do you think this could be one way to motivate, visualize and mobilize your own success?

Any role model who you feel has been successful and whom you can closely watch as you proceed on the path of reaching your very own goal in your life?

Temporarily perhaps for some time initially if you don't mind you can treat me as your role model for the time being.

Try to find out why and how your temporary role model inspires you. When you are faced with a challenge, you can read this role model's life story and see how he dealt with his challenges and how he reached his goal.

Using somewhat such a simple motivational method while you are getting prepared to start your own story can be really inspirational.

Soon you will yourself reach that level, when you can ditch the role model and start consulting your own gut, your own intuition to choose the way to act or react according to your specific circumstances.

The purpose of this role model suggestion of mine is two folds – since this book is a very unconventional one in style and its content.

If for instance I am your temporary role model, the inspirational way may be to quickly glance through my life story and the attached photographs of my personal as well as professional development as shown in this book.

You can closely watch how I have reacted to particular situations and succeeded through them. Likewise you can ask your own inner gut whether there is anything for you to emulate. The decision and choice, of course is entirely your own.

A glance through my life story and its step by step development can also serve as a code of reference.

I supply you with my Success Mantra Tool Kit covering 50 of my own, my personal collection of Mantras, Metaphors, Tools and Attitudes I picked up from my Mentors to suit different challenges at different stages in my life.

You could also witness and feel here a kind of operating systems that I have applied in my own life.

Such a learning, gaining and acting step by step with a cross reference to live photograph at times can be very motivating and invigorating for your own self.

Such cross reference to a true life story can also be instrumental in comparing your own different challenges that you may be facing in your own particular conditions and circumstances of current life.

Therefore, this book is for all people at various levels who want to improve their lives be it Students, Entrepreneurs, Employees, Workers, Managers, Doctors, Journalists, Architects, Scientists and all the people from each and every domain in life who wish to improve their lot – or who are stumbling through one way or the other, or need to create a role model for inspiration and a Mental Tool Kit to which they can refer to from time to time.

It is also a Tool Kit upon which you can fall back for reference and guidance to face your own unique challenges.

Mantra 49

Remember To Gain In Your Life You Always Have To Forego And Sacrifice Some Minimal Comforts

Remember To Gain In Your Life You Always Have To Forego And Sacrifice Some Minimal Comforts.

Even Birds Do It Year After Year.
Life Is Not A Bed Of Roses Without Thorns.

All big discoverers in the world did not simply find the newer lands far away from their homes without consenting to sail with hope and determination. They did so while losing the comforts and the sight of their own shores and homes for reasonably long periods of time.

The more you leave your usual comfort zone, the more you open up to a sea of opportunity.

The more obstacles you may face as temporary setbacks, the more experienced you become on your road to success.

Setbacks may happen temporarily but you will find a solution.

Even competition will try to come in your way – so what?

Be on your job earnestly and the right solution is lying hidden in the problem to be discovered and practiced.

To have guts to see opportunities where other see impossible challenges is visionary leadership, unlike those who indulge in self-victimization as a practice on the other hand.

Even birds use only their own intuition year after year to navigate their long distance flights to warmer regions in Asia and India especially, which is half way around the Globe – that too without any possessions or belongings, without any return assurances, without any food supply security.

They are determined to navigate successfully their way to the breeding grounds in warmer countries.

And are determined also not only to return back home next spring themselves alone but together with their off-springs year after year.

Likewise start believing that you are fortunate to be living in an abundant Universe.

Your efforts will yield results –

- If you think, plan and execute your own strategies in your life.
- On the basis of your own intuition and firm belief that everything you wish in this Universe you can actually acquire.
- If you have faith and perseverance, dream and determination you will watch and enjoy your own small steps and efforts lead you to your own small and later big successes.
- Accumulate small successes day by day until to reach your goal and beyond.
- Stop being depressed – look ahead with hope and your efforts will certainly yield result.
- Think that you are only working on improving whatever situation you are in, you are just doing your Karma with more and more perfection out of your own efforts and your own commitment try doing your better and best.
- You have nothing to lose, only to gain which you will observe yourself.

So, start putting in your best efforts however small to improve your life. And you will see for sure your hard work soon bringing in the rewards you were looking for.

And here let us once again remember the Gospel Truth that

'God Helps Those Who Help Themselves.'

Mantra 50

The 10 Commandments Of Human Relations - The Work Life Balance Mantra

The 10 Commandments Of Human Relations - The Work Life Balance Mantra.

The 10 Commandments of human relations are –

1. Speak to the people. There is nothing as nice as a cheerful word of greetings.
2. Smile at people. It takes 72 muscles to frown, only 14 to smile.
3. Call people by their names.
4. Be friendly and helpful. If you would have friends, be a friend first.
5. Be cordial. Speak and act as if everything you do is a genuine pleasure.
6. Be genuinely interested in people you interact with.
7. Be generous with praise – and cautious with criticism.
8. Be considerate with feelings of others.
9. Be alert while giving service. What counts most in life is what we do for others.
10. Add to this a good sense of humour, a big dose of patience and a dash of humility.

The Work Life Balance Mantra

Successful Companies and their senior officials realize the importance of Work-Life-Balance.

They don't want their people to burn out of exhaustion and even in India though not yet obligatory, many companies have started giving the first and the third Saturday or all Saturdays off to let their people relax and recoup from the hard work they do on 5 days a week nevertheless.

Developing a good working culture by caring for your people and creating a relaxed environment leads to much better results than without it.

For many years ow we started a small Lecture on Vedanta or Kaizen in our offices and factories and the results were astounding.

When we expect growth of your Organization through the time consuming and dedicated efforts of your employees – you must likewise care for the growth and health of their families as well.

Work-Life-Balance therefore means more and more profits and productivity with reduced stress all around us at home and at work place.

Mantra 51

Finally The Master Key For Turbo-Charging Happier And Meaningful Lives Ahead

Finally The Master Key For Turbo-Charging Happier And Meaningful Lives Ahead.

Forget all past grudges and misfortunes, if any.

Stop being a prisoner of any negative past beliefs. Instead become an architect of your positive thoughts and assured success ahead.

For successful people, there are no such things as mistakes and negative circumstances in life. These are only happenings from which you can learn to grow and advance higher on your path of self-mastery.

Expressions of Gratitude, Love, Blessings and Positive Thinking will dissolve all negativity you may have accumulated in yourself with past wrong beliefs.

Totally avoid negative beliefs such as:

I am too young to be a Millionaire

I am too young to be a Leader

I am not smart enough to Lead

I am perhaps too lazy to start on my own

I do not have enough money to start

All these are negative and imaginary beliefs which cannot lead us to success and happiness we righteously yearn for and deserve in our lives.

Make a Fresh Positive Start

If you wish to Unleash

Magical Success in your life ahead

Assume absolute ownership and responsibility for where you stand in your life today and where you wish to rise to.

Close your eyes for a few minutes every morning and visualize and believe what you wish to achieve with your new thoughts and determined efforts.

All current thoughts and the pictures you visualize for your wished and presumed life will manifest.

Follow your bliss with determined efforts.

The Universe will open flood gates for you sooner than later.

You are now the Author of your own Story

You are now the Designer of your Destiny

The Pen is now in your Hands

The Outcome will be

Whatever You Choose.

Stay Blessed

Some Additional Photographs Between 1984 To 2013 For Visualization

RNK with Mr. Justice P.N. Khanna (retired) at the Press Conference with
Mr. Bharat Bhattacharya M.D. State Bank of India 1984

RNK with Inderjit Singh, Chief of Marketing & the State Bank of India,
M.D. Mr. Bharat Bhattacharya and members of the Press - 1984

1st TC Public Issue Press Conference at The Oberoi, New Delhi Ashok Khanna, R.N. Khanna,
Justice P.N. Khanna (Retired) & T.R. Tuli Former Chairman of PNB - 1984

RNK with H.E. Mr. Jacques Chirac, the President of France at ELYSEE Palace in 1985.

A Staff Get-together showing TC's French Directors and Chief Marketing Executive Inder Jit Singh with Chairman Emeritus Mr. Justice P. N. Khanna & Managing Director RNK and Mrs. Khanna at their House

French Minister of Industries H.E. Mr. Noir and the French Ambassador at our Telemecanique & Controls India Ltd. Joint Venture's 1st Plant at Noida Phase I with our Chairman Emeritus Mr. Justice P.N. Khanna, RNK, AK, Mr. Alletru and other Indian & French Directors in January 1986.

1979 Laying The Foundation Stone of Noida Plant with Papa ji, RNK & Rishi at age 6

Rishi & Radhika with Mr. Terasaki at his house in Osaka Japan 1982

Mr & Mrs. R N Khanna with an Indo Japanese Trade Promotion Delegation

The Family with Jurgen Schmidt at C-69, Friends Colony 1992

Mr. Y. Terasaki, President of our Technical Collaborators Terasaki Electric of Japan with our Managing Director RNK at his office - 1981

RNK with German Chancellor Mr. Helmul Kohl at C&S Stall
at ELECRAMA - 1986.

At Elecrama Seminar in New Delhi – 2004
Rishi, Ashok, Werner & Jurgen Schmitz of AVK Seg & RNK - 2004

Anuj, Rishi , Komishke, Ashok, Dr Hollunder & RNK at our Stall in Elecrama 2002 in Bombay

RNK and Mrs. Kanwal Khanna with Mr. & Mrs. Fancisco Grazia & Family in 2006

Rishi and RNK at the Krupp Maks Diesel Engine Plant and Kiel Germany with our CEO AVK, Dr. S K Gupta and Mr. Komishke, Director of Krupp Mak

Our Chairman RNK in his Capacity as Chairman of the Indo-Spanish and Indo-Portuguese Joint Business Councils of FICCI, delivering his Welcome Address to H.E. Prof. Anibal Cavaco Silva, the President of Portugal at the Indo-Portuguese Joint Business Council organized together by FICCI, CII & Assochem at the Taj Palace Hotel New Delhi – 2007

Our Chairman RNK was conferred the rare Gold Medal and the Rare Distinguished Alumnus Award 2006 for his Outstanding Achievement and Contribution to the Electrical Industry in India at the convocation of IIT-Kharagpur, in presence of IIT-Director In charge Dr. Acharya and the Chief Executive of Vodafone-India Mr. Anil Sarin, who also received this Award the same day. In 2007, IIT-Kharagpur also recognised RNK as a "Jewel in the Crown of IIT-Kharagpur".

H.E. Mr. Pranab Mukherjee, then the Union Minister of Commerce & Finance, now the Hon. President of India, presenting the "Industrialist of The HYear 2008 Award"with a citation to RNK for his outstanding contribution to the Indian industry with FICCI President Mr. Lalit Mehra

Our illustrious young Managing Directors Aditya (Electrical Engg. & Chartered Accountant) and Rishi & Anuj Khanna both Electrical and Electronic Engg. and MBAs assume responsibilities for phenomenal growth ahead.

Honouring & Distributing trophies to our valued Dealers at a Dealers Meeting in Kathmandu

Our Senior Officials M/s. S C Nagpal, A Gulati , R C Jain & P P Singh with RNK, Ashok at a Dealers Meet in Chennai. Our Dealers are a very valuable part of our Extended Family for almost 5 Decades now

C&S Cricket Team Winners-1983 with our Chairman Emeritus Mr. Justice P.N. Khanna standing from left to right showing Aditya, Anju, Radhika, Rishi, Kanwal, Anuj, RNK, VK Sharma, PP Singh, AK and others.

RNK as president of Elecrama 2004 welcoming the Honourable then The Home Minister of India Mr. Lal Krishan Adwani ji

Then the Union Law Minister Mr. Arun Jaitly addressing Elecrama 2004

RNK as president of Elecrama 2004 at his Inaugural Address

Elecrama 2004 was the Largest Elecrama Till then where thousands of companies from India and Overseas participated successful setting a Benchmark for Future Elecramas

With our Dearest Beeji & Papaji on our common Birthday The 28th January 2002, 90th for him and 62nd for RNK

2007 Bhagwat at C-69, Friends Colony with our revered Guruji and the entire Family.

RNK & Kanwal in the Procession at The 7 Day long Sh. Bhagwat Katha at Guruvayoor in Kerala with our revered Gurujee Sh. Venugopal Goswamiji, Family & Friends

The family together at dear Radhika Ajay Wedding in 1994 together with Krishanji and Ushaji.

50th Anniversary Celebration 28th January 2016

The 50th Anniversary Celebration

The 50th Anniversary Celebration Desk

Mr. Rajiv Puri welcoming at the 50th Anniversaruy Guests

The Khanna family on 28th January 2006 at the 40th Anniversary of C&S at our Farm House "Tranquility" Sohna.

The Khanna Family Get-together at the 100th Birthday of our revered Papajee at C-69, Friends Papajee, Sati, Reeti, Subhash, Rama, Uma & Amit Standing – Radhika, Ajay, Sunil Timma, Karishma,

Founder's Day Luncheon at Farm House "Tranquility" Sohna (2011)

Colony duly blessed by Gurujee standing behind him, sitting Bailu, Anil, Anju, Ashok, Kanwal, Ravi Anuj, Shaila, Guruji, Suneeta, Atul, Geeta, Akshay, Aditya Priya, Divya Rishi, Ushaji & Tina

The C&S Family Arriving at the 50th Anniversary

Celebration at the Tranquility Farm on the 28th January 2016

RNK Addressing the CS extended family of Senior Managers at the 50th

Anniversary Celebrations of our Company on 28/1/2016 at Tranquility in Sohna

We have a Dream
We have a Dream

Rama Kanwal, RNK, Ashok, Anju with Uma & Joginderji

The Team is Rocking at the 50th Anniversary Celebrations

Ashok, Anju, Kanwal, RNK, Uma & Rama

The Team is Rocking at the 50th Anniversary Celebrations

Elecrama 2016 - Bangalore

Elecrama 2010 - Mumbai

Elecrama 2014 - Bangalore

Dealers Meet at Dubai

Ms. Nirmala Sitharaman, then the Hon'ble Minister of Commerce & Industry and Minister of State for Finance and Corporate Affairs very kindly visiting our stall at Hannover Fair 2015 alongwith officials of the ministry to view our stall at Hannover Messe witness our Make in India products, which we export to 85 countries around the globe.

Our Smart and most Competent officials at the Hannover Fair 2015

Our managing director, Mr. Rishi Nath Khanna alongwith BHEL Chairman Mr. B. Prasada Rao and other Indian Industry Leader, Part of Top 10 Indian CEO Delegation selected by Govt. of India addressing a seminar on Make in India Opportunities in Electronics and Electrical Sectors at Hannover 2015, inaugurated by Hon'ble Prime Minister Mr. Narendra Modi together with the Hon'ble German Chancellor Mrs. Angela Merkel.

Our Stall at Hannover Fair, Germany - 2015

With Our GM (HR) Devashish Kumar and
Sunil Dwivedi (Projects CSR)

Serve Samman, an initiative to promote vocational education & training among underprivileged children and women with our Managing Director Mr. Aditya Khanna, our H.R. Head Mr. Rajiv Puri & Mr. Deepak Khanna.

Our Chairman RNK's visit in March 2016 to address the children of the Him Jyoti Vocational Institute, Dehradun founded & mentored by Hon'ble Mr. Sudarshan Agarwal, former Governor of Uttarkhand & Sikkim, where our Company has been providing support for the education of 15 Girls from the economically weaker sections of the Society. Sitting along RNK are Ms. Jyoti Dhawan, Principal-Him Jyoti School and Ms. Juhi M. Garg, Principal-Him Jyoti Vocational Training Institute.

Our Director Radhika looks after our CSR Activities where we are increasingly becoming more involved in skill Development in under privileged areas.

Radhika, Ajay, Nyrah, RNK, Veer, Divya, Jai, Kanwal & Rishi at C-69, Friends Colony in 2014

Kanwal, Radhika, Ravi at Kasauli October - 2015

Ravi, Kanwal and Ashi on our 50th Anniversary at Mussoorie 2017

Deepawali 2017 Poojan at Home Mandir

Enjoying the sunshine bonding with close family and friends on our 50th anniversary on 11 December 2017 in the snow peaked Mussoorie Hills,

getting back to my roots where my own tryst with destiny and childhood dream started shaping up 70 long years ago after the partition of India in 1947.

An Addressal to My Aspiring Readers

Chapter 15

AN ADDRESSAL TO MY ASPIRING READERS

My Dear aspiring readers,

It is my pleasure to reach each one of you from all walks of life. You may be young, younger or older. You may be a student with any university or college or faculty. You may be from the IIT's or the Business Schools or a graduate from any other stream, you may be an optimist from any walk of life.

This book therefore is primarily intended to be my humble little contribution towards the success of all those daring optimists, salf starters entrepreneurs or for millions of all those others who may also choose to accomplish substantial and quantum jumps and gains in their own lives or carriers ahead in whatever activity position or profession they may be engaged in their lives today.

The devotedly chosen relaxed style of this book, the diligently compiled write-ups and comments, and above all the carefully hand-picked '51 Golden Mantras or the Tools in my Tool Kit' will precipitate the Universal Goodness into your lives and those of your loved ones.

So relax, enjoy and make this book your constant companion or a ready reckoner for all your dilemmas and doubts. Have faith in yourself and in the simple and true wisdom of this book.

My foremost dream today is – to witness the utmost happiness, health and well-being of each and every one of you.

I do hope that some words of acquired wisdom which I have shared with you through this book will get disseminated and practiced upon in your lives – to build a more beautiful life for each and every one of you ahead.

Chapter 16

C&S AT A GLANCE AS I SEE IT TODAY

IN 2019

Today I can say with a sense of accomplishment that my continuing journey 'From Garage To The Globe' has been quite a successful one. We have attained benchmarks in scale and scope, we have triumphed over the test of times and tides. We have sustained through quality and quantity and we have accomplished many feats – with a hope that there are more to come.

With a World Class product range and employing the best technologies, we do hope that in the next five years the C&S Group should have a projected turnover 50 percent of which shall be exports.

With our Research and Development (R&D) team of 100 engineers working dedicatedly in our Govt. of India approved R&D centres we keep designing new products. We reinvent product processes and even revamp many products acquired from our own overseas collaborators. As a result many of our partners have found some of our products more cost effective with better performance than their existing ones available worldwide.

Having said so, I feel the highest point of satisfaction is our team. Our squad comprising excellent engineers (many IIT-ians), technocrats, managers and technicians have worked with all their hearts and heads to bring us where we stand today.

We have been, I must admit, extremely successful in choosing our bunch, or they have been exceptional in their choice! We compete with the best.

C&S fully realizes the social responsibilities it shoulders towards building up a better tomorrow for the Nation. Our CSR (Corporate Social Responsibility) initiatives have continually reinforced the long sighted vision of strengthening India's social infrastructural and Skill development.

Our 'Power Community Power Youth' program aims at developing skill sets among unemployed youth to make them self-dependent. Under our 'Empower Women' program women from the marginalized section of society are taught various skills to increase their employability.

Our 'Power for Kids' program supports the under-privileged children with their education and further generating employment skills. 'Power for Health' is another initiative under which communities/hospitals/schools are supported with latest technology installations for self-reliance in eco-friendly power generation.

With a vision to support our eco-system and the preservation of flora, fauna and biological demographics the C&S has notably contributed to the 'Clean Ganga' and 'Tiger Conservation' projects, among others.

With a wish to grow
With you by our side
I hope we shall continue to crusade,
Creating tides in the years ahead,
Success being a journey not a destination to stop.

Stay Blessed, Loved and Protected

Ravi - Ravinder Nath Khanna